How To
Buy Land
CHEAP

4th Edition

D0809078

T1NR1E

T3NR1W

T2NR1E

T2NR1W

T2NR2W

T1NR1E

T1NR1R

T1NR2W

T1SR1E

T1SR1W

T1SR2W

Edward Preston

COMPLETELY REVISED AND EXPANDED

Loompanics Unlimited
Port Townsend, Washington

HOW TO BUY LAND CHEAP, 4th Edition
© 1977 by Boggle Publications
© 1981, 1984, 1991 by Loompanics Unlimited
Printed in USA

Published by:
Loompanics Unlimited
PO Box 1197
Port Townsend, WA 98368

Illustrations by Laurel Marotta

ISBN 1-55950-064-6
Library of Congress
   Catalog Card Number 91-060105

CONTENTS

PREFACE

Every year I get cards, letters and photos from people who have used this book to buy land for less than the cost of a night out. I've heard from people, not only in the United States, but all over the world, who've used the information presented here to buy houses for a few hundred dollars. Nothing makes my day more than opening the mail to find yet another account of how *you* bought land cheap.

It has been 14 years since the first edition of ***How to Buy Land Cheap***. You would think all the cheap land would have been scooped up, and a lot of it has been. But as old sources dry up, new sources sprout. Old fashioned homesteading is a thing of the past — but now there's Urban Homesteading. The U.S. Bureau of Land Management sells less land every year, but the Savings & Loan Bailout has brought a bonanza of bargain-basement buying opportunities. The most reliable source of cheap land — tax foreclosed property — continues to produce, though the best areas have shifted a little.

In 14 years, **How to Buy Land Cheap** has grown from a small pamphlet to an impressive resource for bargain hunters. I've seen a lot of expensive imitations of this book come and go. I buy them, read them, and follow-up on the best advice they offer. But far and away my best source of information is you — fellow travelers in the search for dirt cheap. I hope you enjoy this edition, and that you tell me about your finds. Please write to me in care of Loompanics Unlimited and I will try to include *your* story in the next edition of **How to Buy Land Cheap**.

Unitl next time, happy hunting!

Edward Preston
January 1991

- 1 -

OUR BIG
LAND GRAB

I grabbed the letter out of the mailbox and ran upstairs, opening it on the way. "It came," I yelled to my wife. "It's here... look at it... it's ours!" I held up a piece of paper and waved it around the room. It took us five minutes to settle down enough to look at it. And what was this incredible document? A million dollar inheritance? One of my stories sold to the movies? Had we won first prize in one of those contests I was always entering? Nope. It was a *Quit Claim Deed* to eight town lots in Daniels County, Montana. Three of the lots were in the town of Navajo (population seven) and five were in Peerless (population 125). The total price for our enormous "estate" was $25.00. It cost $5.00 more to have the deed recorded and to get maps of the two towns. A total of $30.00 for the whole works. The lots are standard size town lots — 35 x 140 feet. The taxes come to $7.48 a year.

We handled the entire business ourselves — through the mail. No closing fees, no lawyer's fee, no real estate agent's fee. How? It couldn't have been simpler. I wrote to the County Treasurer (I didn't even know his name) of Daniels County, c/o County Courthouse, Scobey, Montana. Scobey is the county seat, where all the county business is taken care of and where the county offices are. It's easy to find the county seat if you have an atlas: Right next to it is a dot in a circle or a small black square (see Figure 1-1). You need to have an atlas for this — often road maps don't show the county seat.

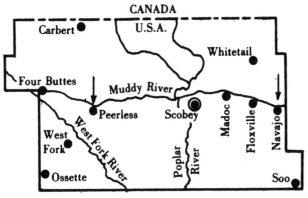

Figure 1-1

A map of Daniels County, Montana. Scobey, the County Seat, is indicated by a dot in a circle. The arrows show the towns where the author bought a total of eight lots for the sum of $25.00.

What did I write? I asked if they had any property for sale for back taxes and they sent me a long list. We bought these particular lots because they were the cheapest. Since some of the tax lots to be had in Daniels County cost only a few dollars and some cost several thousand, I sent the list back and asked them to put a check mark beside the ones that had buildings on them. Sure enough, the expensive ones had buildings, and the County Treasurer was even kind enough to describe them as "house," "building," or "shack." We didn't buy any of these (there was so much to choose from) but it did give us a good picture of what was available.

This all happened many years ago, and we've never been to Montana to check on our "Empire," but we still get a kick out of looking at the deeds and the maps. We may never live on it, though we hope to see it someday, *but still it is ours!* And believe me, very few thrills can match that of owning land.

Let's backtrack and look at the steps that led up to our Land Grab. I just happened to hit it with Daniels County, but I wrote the same basic letter to many other counties who didn't answer at all. So it isn't always that easy. Still, keep in mind that there is plenty of tax-foreclosed property throughout this country that can be bought cheap *if you know how.* That is what this book is for — to show you step-by-step just how to find it, where to find it, and how to buy it. Read on.

- 2 -
DECIDING WHAT YOU WANT AND NEED

Before you start writing hundreds of letters to County Treasurers all over the country, do some thinking that can save you a lot of time and postage. Why do you want to buy land cheap? If you are a land speculator or a land dreamer like me, then it doesn't matter much what kind of land you buy or where it is — just as long as it's cheap. There is a lot of pleasure to be had just by owning land. We know we have a place to go that is ours, no matter what happens in the future. True, there's nothing there but some dirt, but we could park an RV on it or camp on it or someday build a house on it.

Land Dreaming

For those living in small apartments that cost hundreds of dollars a month in rent, it's fun to buy land somewhere for less than a night on the town (even if you eat at McDonalds). Many cold winter evenings can be spent looking at maps and deeds, dreaming about the wild west or the rugged northeast and what it would be like to live there. Of course, you are going to dream about building a house on your land. And some day, you just might — because most of the great things we do started as dreams a long time ago and slowly became more and more real.

One man who read this book bought a piece of land as a gift for his wife. It cost $50 altogether, so it wasn't a really expensive gift. But it brought his wife more pleasure than just about any gift he'd ever given her. She loved being a landowner. She loved the feeling of knowing there was some spot on the world that was hers. She spent hours looking at maps, thinking about the land, planning a trip to go plant flowers there.

Speculating

There's another reason for buying cheap land: speculation. While most worthless land is doomed to stay that way, it's hard to imagine a $10 parcel going down in value (and who cares if it does?). But there are many possibilities for it to suddenly become valuable. One person who bought land with the help of this book got paid by an oil company for allowing them to drill on his land. It wasn't much money, but if they *had* struck oil, he would have struck it rich.

You never know when they're going to decide to run a freeway through your land. If they do, you can make a handsome profit selling it to the government. Your land may become an important parcel for other reasons: the neighbors need it, or some valuable commodity like gold or water is discovered there, or a big manufacturer decides to locate a plant nearby. You never know when property will boom in value, and you aren't likely to go bust with land this cheap. But I don't want to get your hopes up too much, because any land you buy for less than $100 is likely to never be worth much to anyone (except you).

Recreation

Another reason to buy land cheap is recreation. Some people like camping and hiking and would rather be on their own land than in a state park or official campground. If you can buy land in beautiful country cheap enough, you can actually save money from what it might cost for a nearby campground. If you enjoy the RV lifestyle, what could be better than owning small parcels all over the country where you can park your rig and settle-in whenever you want? No more "reservations required," or being turned away from a full RV park when you're tired of driving, or paying outrageous fees for a place to park your vehicle.

If you are looking for land for recreational purposes, then you have many options. Of course, you'll probably want land in the areas that you most enjoy staying, so you should concentrate your search in those areas. One thing you'll need is *access* to your land. A lot of the cheapest land available does not have access: there is no road that goes anywhere near the property. In some cases, you might have to get permission from a neighbor to cross their property to get to yours. If you find land that you like, but that doesn't have access, you will want to resolve the access problem *before* you buy it.

I know a man in Michigan who bought land just to have a place for his large family to spend some fun weekends. He lived and worked in Detroit as an engineer. The land he bought was an abandoned gravel pit a few hours away in the country. He turned the gravel pit into a man-made lake and stocked it with bass. He made a crude dirt road into the property and leveled an area for putting-up tents and for a volleyball field. He put in an outhouse and that was it: a perfect little retreat for summer weekends and for his grown kids to use.

A Cheap Home

For some people, buying cheap land is more than entertainment or speculation — it means an entire change of life. Karl Henck used *How To Buy Land Cheap* to find a new home. He first wrote to governments in Maine, Vermont and New York State. Washington County, New York, had 24 parcels for sale by sealed bid auction. Karl bid on four of them (sight unseen) and was high bidder on two. Here's what happened next:

"I inspected the properties; one was adjacent to railroad tracks, the other was on an old town road, wooded and hilly. I forfeited my 20% deposit on the railroad property and came up with the rest of the $680 I needed to buy the other piece. It's about one

acre. I built a small log cabin and have been here ever since. Your book made it all possible."

If you are after cheap land in hopes of finding an inexpensive place to live, then you need to do a little more research. The first big question is: How are you going to make a living once you get there? Most cheap land is located in depressed areas that people have been moving *away* from, where unemployment is high. If you haven't got a job lined up in advance, you'd better have a good bankroll to tide you over.

While land is cheap in certain places, the jobs available don't pay that well, either. This brings up another point: How well suited are you to small town life? Most cheap land is in remote areas. Country living can be quite different from city living — and that's what attracts so many people to the rural lifestyle. But living in remote areas can be hard, too. If you've lived in a New York City apartment all your life, it might take some time to adjust to living where the elements can play havoc with your life (severe heat or cold, snows, flooding, etc.).

There are a number of good books that deal with what it's like living in remote or rural America. One is called *The Eden Seeker's Guide*, by Bill Seavey, available from Loompanics Unlimited. It describes some of the most beautiful places in the world for people to live. And it provides a lot of information on what different lifestyles are like and how to prepare to make a big life change like this. Other guides are included in the *Other Helpful Information* chapter at the end of this book.

If you are independently wealthy or retired or have a source of income you can take anywhere, then you don't have to worry about finding a job. You may have other concerns, though. You may be raising a family and want your children to have access to quality schools. Or you might not want to live in a town that doesn't have a hospital. Once you find a place that has cheap land, you will want to make further inquiries with the local Chamber of Commerce to determine what amenities are available.

Once you have some idea what you want to do with your land, and what you need to make your life there comfortable, it will make the search for cheap land a lot easier.

- 3 -

STARTING YOUR SEARCH

Ready to start? All right, if you don't have an atlas, buy one. If you can't, borrow one from a library or a friend. Think about where you would like to own land: "Out West," "Down South," "New England," or anywhere. Start with a large general area and narrow it down. First, eliminate resort and heavy industry areas. Those areas probably won't have any cheap land for sale. But don't take this for granted. If you're dead set on getting cheap land in a certain area, then even if it seems like the last place in the world to find it, keep trying. Keep nosing around, asking questions, checking with county treasurers and city real estate departments. You might just find what you're looking for, *if you keep at it.*

Now you've got the atlas. Pore over that book. Look at lightly settled areas: non-industrial, not on the seashore or near a lake, dam, or ski resort. Then find out how the people in that region make a living. Is it mainly farm land? Desert land? Swamp? If the atlas doesn't give enough information, ask your local librarian to help you pick some books that throw more light on the subject.

Since most of the cheap land available is in lightly settled areas, you would likely be looking for a small town to live in or near. If this is your interest, then I recommend the *Capsule Descriptive Digest of Small-Town, USA*, published by Woods Creek Press. This guide includes descriptions of more than 40 small towns that are perfect for people who want to get out of the big city. Each description of a town includes history, climate, real estate, utilities, taxes, employment, communications, medical facilities and health services, schools and churches, transportation, recreation, shopping, services and restaurants, points of interest, organizations and clubs, visitor accommodations, and other items. You get the *whole* picture of what life in each town is like.

The *Capsule Descriptive Digest of SmallTown, USA* is an excellent reference guide for those trying to find a nice place to live where land might be cheap. If you already know where you want to live, you can write to Woods Creek Press and see if their digest includes any small towns in your chosen area. The digest is $6.00 from:

Woods Creek Press
809 N Sanders Ave
Ridgecrest, CA 93555

I also recommend the *Rural Property Bulletin* as a real estate guide to the rural United States. It looks like

a classified shopper for rural property hunters, and
lists a good deal of inexpensive land. The bulletin
comes out monthly. Subscriptions are $12.00. A sample
issue can be had for $1.00 from:

> Rural Property Bulletin
> P.O. Box 4331
> Prescott, AZ 86302

One of the best resources when starting your search
are the free farm catalogs. Not only can you learn a lot
from farm catalogs about what is available and what
is happening in the area you're interested in, but they
are terrific Wish Books — like the Sears catalog of 50
years ago. Don't be put off because you think they list
only farms for sale. They have every kind of property
you can think of, and a picture for almost every listing.

There are three big companies that send out free
catalogs or brochures upon request:

> United Farm Agency
> 612 W 47 St
> Kansas City, MO 64112

7/15/95 FORWARDING
ORDER EXPIRED

> Strout Realty, Inc
> Plaza Towers
> Springfield, MO 65804

> American Farm Digest
> PO Box 5177
> St. Louis, MO 63139

The first two are huge real estate agencies. United Farm has over 500 sales offices throughout the U.S. Strout has nearly the same number. Both offer hundreds of listings of all types of property in every state. The *American Farm Digest* is a monthly publication with listings from dozens of different real estate companies all across the United States.

The land advertised in these catalogs is *not* tax foreclosed property, so don't expect to find lots for $2.00 apiece or a house for $100.00. You may buy nothing from the farm companies (we never did), but you can soak up real information that you can use later on. We found local agents of both Strout and United to be sincere and helpful. They didn't hesitate to answer numerous questions by mail, and they were very honest about pointing out shortcomings in certain properties. We never felt that they were just out to *sell!* They looked upon us as possible future neighbors. There is something else, too: If they think you are solid and sincere, their word at the local bank could carry some weight if you ever apply for a mortgage. Outside large cities, personal recommendation still means something.

This is interesting, you say, but isn't it just a waste of time? What do I need catalogs for? Can't I just go ahead and write the counties now? Sure you can, but send for the catalogs, too. There are some things you can *learn* from them, and later when you buy your land, you will be grateful for every bit of information you picked up along the way. And you won't have to say, "Why didn't somebody *tell* me this?"

Look in the catalogs for areas where homes (houses on lots) sell for less than $10,000. These are good areas for exploring further in your search for cheap land. These towns were probably cut off when a new highway was built and have been quietly losing population for years. Maybe a new town has grown up near the new highway, leaving the old one out of the way. But this could be a bonanza for you. The old town probably has a half dozen old one-family frame houses for a few thousand apiece.

For a couple thousand more, you can probably buy the town's White Elephant — the Victorian grand mansion that was originally built for the town banker or doctor. It spent a few decades as a rooming house, and is now abandoned and neglected. The trimmings are usually of sculptured cast iron, and inside you will find carved mantlepieces, mahogany staircases, parquet floors, stained glass windows, and other details that would cost a fortune to duplicate today. These old "monsters" can turn out to be real treasures. Dollar for dollar, they are among the best housing buys in America.

We even found a 23-room house in Eastport, Maine, that was even older than the type I described. This one was built for the Commanding General of the British Expeditionary Forces in the War of 1812. It had a fireplace in almost every room, and the original details were intact. The price was $11,500, which figures out to $500 a room. We didn't buy it because we couldn't figure out how to make a living in Eastport, Maine. But there it was — not only cheap, but available on easy terms, too. There are houses like this, if not quite as large or historical, in small towns all over the country.

Once you've found a promising area, it's a good idea to get the local newspaper. Go to the library and ask to look at the *Gales Directory* (every library has one). Look up the newspapers in the vicinity and send off $1.00 for a sample copy. Most small town newspapers come out once a week. If there is a daily paper available, ask for the Sunday edition. Mail your request to the Circulation Editor. You won't need an address — just the name of the paper and the town.

In about one week to ten days, you'll get your paper. Compare the listings in the paper with those in the farm catalogs. This will give you a good idea of real estate values in town (though you may be able to find land much cheaper than the stuff you see advertised — read on). The Help Wanted ads will give you a good idea about work opportunities. The ads will tell you about various services available, who the large employers are, whether there are schools or not, what churches are located nearby, what sort of entertainment is available, etc.

The papers can tell you other things, too. If you want to live in the country for free, look for an ad asking for a "caretaker." You might spot one, or you can put an ad in yourself saying that you are available. Often, the owners are away and just want somebody to take care of the place. You might live in a cottage on the grounds or in the main house itself. You would get free rent and you might even get paid. If you're not ready to buy land yet, or simply can't afford it at any price, this is the next best thing.

Or suppose you are ready to buy, have a little money saved, and are looking around. It could be that the counties you're interested in have no tax delinquent property at all. Put an ad in the largest regional paper (try the local paper, too) telling exactly what you're looking for. You will get a pretty good idea of what you want when you describe it in words.

Another thing. If the catalog offerings are medium to high in price, and the descriptions keep repeating that the schools are excellent, and that there are several colleges within a few miles — do some further checking. This county might have low property taxes but very high school taxes, something you might not have thought of at all.

It is also worth calling the phone company to have them send you a local phone book for the area you are interested in. It will come in about 10 days to two weeks, and the couple bucks it costs will be added to your next phone bill. By looking through the Yellow Pages, you can get an idea of what goods and services are available in that area — important information if you are thinking of moving there.

- 4 -
BUYING LAND CHEAP
FROM
COUNTY GOVERNMENTS

Tax Lands

Now let's go back to the land that counties sell cheap — usually at auction for back taxes. Remember, only counties and cities have real estate taxes. There are no state or federal real estate taxes. The county officials, the tax assessor, treasurer, clerk and recorder are the people who hold the keys to the ownership of tax property. They know what is available and what is likely to come up for auction in the future. We have heard so much lately about official corruption in high and low places that you might think these officials expect to be paid off, but it isn't so. I have found almost all county officials to be honest, dedicated and impartial people.

They are your sources for buying land cheap and here is how you get in touch with them: write the letter shown in Figure 4-1 to the County Treasurer of the county or counties where you are interested in buying property. My advice is to blanket the area. Write letters to every county in that region. Use the form letter in Figure 4-1 as your guide (this letter will also be useful when writing to federal and state government agencies listed in the next two chapters).

Your Name
Your Street Address
Your City, State, Zip Code

Date

County Treasurer
... County
County Court House
City, State, Zip Code

Dear Sir or Madam,

   Please send me information about real estate in your jurisdiction which might be auctioned off for back taxes or any other reason (surplus to your needs, etc.).

   I am also interested in information on property which might be for sale on a Quit Claim Deed.

   If you keep a mailing list for notification of real estate auctions or sales, would you please add my name or send me an application for adding my name to the list?

Thank you for your assistance.

Sincerely,

(Signature)

Figure 4-1

*A sample form letter to use when writing to
county governments in search of cheap land.*

After you have put all those letters in the mail, you will have a few weeks before the replies start coming in. You can fill the time looking at the farm catalogs and re-reading this book (while you are biting your nails). You might also want to read some of the items listed in the *Other Helpful Information* section at the back of this book.

Some answers will come back right away, usually within a couple of weeks; others will take three to four months. Some counties won't answer at all, so after six months put a NA (No Answer) beside their name on your list. If you don't have a list, make one. Next to each county you should write the date you sent your letter, and the date of their answer, or an NA next to that. You can also put in a short description of the kind of answer you get, and the date of their next auction. This short rundown can tell you at a glance where you're at in the land buying business.

Don't expect the County Treasurer to answer immediately with a list of properties you can buy for peanuts. It is possible, of course, but there are quite a few other responses you can get, too. Here are some sample types of responses you can expect and how you should handle them:

Response: "The land auction was already held this year, and there won't be another one until next spring. It will be announced, along with a listing of delinquent properties, for three issues preceding the sale in the *(name of the local paper)*."

What To Do: Send $1.00 to the local paper they name (you don't need the street address) and ask them to send you a copy of the paper that has the next county land auction announcement. Don't worry about the date. Local papers are very good about this.

Response: "We don't hold auctions of tax delinquent property, nor do we have a list of it. However, if you should be in the vicinity, you might drop in and I will show you the deeds for properties that are available. Should you be interested in some of it, I could inform you of the procedures for acquiring it."

What To Do: If you get a letter like that, go there if you can. Plan a trip to include several neighboring counties while you are at it. Some counties have a policy of not foreclosing on property (taking it away from the owner) unless somebody comes along and wants it. Here is where the impression you make on the county officials can mean something in your favor or against it. They don't expect you to appear in a business suit and tie, but if you crawl out of a van at 8 a.m. looking unwashed, unslept and generally scroungy, don't expect them to be very friendly. For your benefit, look neat and make a good impression.

Response: "We have put your name on our mailing list and we will mail you an announcement of our next auction."

What To Do: Just wait. Meanwhile, write to other counties in the area and try to work out a plan to visit their auctions, too.

Response: "We do not have any tax delinquent property for auction."

What To Do: Try them again in a year or two.

Response: "We do not have any such property at the moment."

What To Do: This means that they *do* have some from time to time, so write to them every six months or so.

Response: "We do not decide when the tax sales are to be held. That is up to the county auditor to decide. The last one was three years ago."

What To Do: Write to the County Auditor and ask them to put your name on their mailing list if they have one. Include a stamped envelope with your own address on it. Later, write the County Treasurer again anyway.

As I said earlier, you will get many different kinds of responses, but most of them will sound like one or another of the examples above.

Auctions

Now let's go back and take a look at the first sentence of the letter you sent to the county treasurers (Figure 4-1) where you asked about property to be sold at auction for back taxes. Suppose that a number of county treasurers answered, telling you exactly when and where their next auction would be. You don't always have to be there in person. Some counties will let you send in sealed bids. (This means that they don't open the envelopes with the bids in them until the auction.) Still, there are some auctions you do have to go to. In that case, get there early. At least *two days* early. Make an expedition out of it and your work will pay off for you.

Locating The Property

The list of properties will arrive several weeks before the auction. The County Treasurer will send it to you, or the local paper will send you a clipping of the announcement, with full details — except one. You will discover a maddening fact. Usually these properties will not have a street address. They will be described like this: "Great Lot 2, Div. 8, Lot 5, bounded North by road, South by Presb. Ch., East by Poffrey, West by Rt. 217."

You will look at this, and at the *upset price* (minimum starting bid) and say, "Gee, this looks interesting, but how am I supposed to find it?" That is the reason I advise you to go a few days early. Go to the County Treasurer's office and ask if you can buy a *plat map* (a map that shows where these parcels really are) so you can find them and look at them.

The plat map costs a few dollars and they're worth every penny of it. You can take the maps, locate the properties you are interested in bidding on, and drive around the county looking at them.

A typical description for ten acres might read something like this: SW ¼ SE ¼ SE ¼ Sec 15, T15N R21W. Looks like gibberish, doesn't it? In fact, it's a system of map coordinates that allow you to pinpoint the piece of property being discussed. Let me explain how it works.

Given the intersection of two main roads, one going east/west (the baseline), the other north/south (the meridian), all the land in the nearby vicinity can be mapped out using the intersection as a starting point for a grid. Figure 4-2 shows the grid formed by a baseline and meridian. In our description, above, T15N stands for TOWNSHIP 15 NORTH which is the 15th township north of the baseline. R21W stands for RANGE 21 WEST which is the 21st township west of the meridian. These two coordinates tell you exactly where the township is in relation to the intersection of the meridian and the baseline.

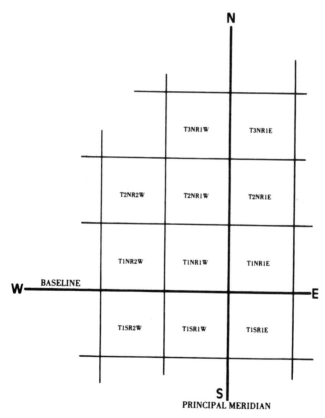

Figure 4-2

How to identify and locate a township.

Once you have located the township, it is easy to locate the specific land. A standard township is six miles long and six miles wide, for a total of 36 square miles. A "section" is one square mile. Therefore, there are 36 sections in a township, and they are numbered as shown in Figure 4-3. In our description, we are looking for section 15 ("Sec 15").

STANDARD TOWNSHIP: 36 SECTIONS

6	5	4	3	2	1
7	8	9	10	11	12
18	17	16	15★	14	13
19	20	21	22	23	24
30	29	28	27	26	25
31	32	33	34	35	36

← 6 MILES →

Figure 4-3

Each township is divided into 36 sections, as shown. This is township T15N R21W (our example township). Section 15 is indicated with a star.

Each section contains 640 acres. The rest of the description above refers to compass directions within the section (SW = southwest, SE = southeast, etc.). The fractions refer to portions of the section. SW ¼ SE ¼ SE ¼ translates to the southwest quarter of the southeast quarter of the southeast quarter of the section. I know that probably still sounds confusing, but if you look at Figure 4-4, it should all make sense. A little study and practice will help you to be able to visualize the location of almost any rural property.

Even with maps, you will probably have to ask the neighbors to help you find some places. In a way, that is good. You get to meet the people who could one day be your neighbors. Most of them will be friendly and can give you pointers about the property you are interested in. They can tell you things you never thought of. This is not to scare you off — most of the time they are just being open and helpful. You will run into a closed-mouth one once in a while, but not often.

While you're driving around the county, you can also pick up other bits of information — such as how high the school taxes are, how far it is to the nearest work center, and so on.

Easement and Access

When evaluating the land you want to bid on, there are two big things to watch out for: easement and access. *Easement* means that somebody else (maybe the County Highway Department or power company) has the right to cross the property. *Access* means that you can reach the land directly without having to go through someone else's property to get there. If you're not sure, ask the County Treasurer, and you might also ask the neighbors. This is one thing you should straighten out before you bid. If you don't, you might have problems later.

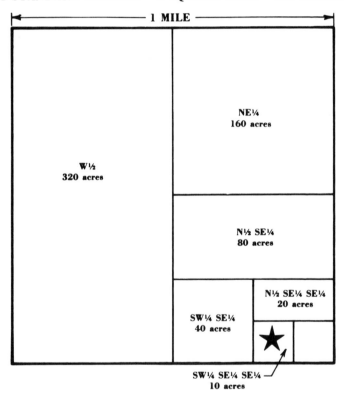

1 STANDARD SECTION = 1 SQUARE MILE = 640 ACRES

Figure 4-4

This map shows how a standard section of a township is divided for land identification purposes. The parcel of land in our example, SW ¼ SE ¼ SE ¼, is indicated with a star.

Buying Before the Auction

If you want to get the jump on everybody, follow my advice. Go to the county and start checking everything out a few days early. After you have the plat map and have found the tax properties that are to be auctioned, *you don't have to wait until the auction!* There is no law that says you can't go directly to the owners and make a deal. You could offer to pay the back taxes in exchange for part of the property (maybe it is a farm with several houses and barns).

If you go to the auction, others might outbid you. But if you can make a deal before the auction, *you are in.* So, if you see a place you really want, go ahead and make an offer to the owner. You have nothing to lose.

Bidding

It pays to do your homework. When you get to the auction, you will find that most of the people bidding against you are local people — and believe me, *they* have done their homework. They might have had their eye on a piece of land for years and have been saving up to bid on it if it ever came up for auction. That is the kind of competition you might get, so be prepared.

At the auction, you're tense and excited. You notice that the bids are running pretty steep — way above the minimums — and that worries you. A piece of land you are interested in comes up. You put in an early bid and you're so excited your voice squeaks. A moment later your bid is topped and it goes on, out of your range.

This happens two more times and you are about ready to give up.

Then a tract comes up that you thought of as only mildly interesting because of certain problems — too far out in the country, too many rocks, an old, burned-out house. But now that the other pieces are gone, this one suddenly looks like an estate. You bid. Someone tops it. You bid again. Silence. *Whaddaya know, it's yours!* Let your breath out. You feel like you have just won a cross-country race. It is yours! But is it? There's a catch.

Redemption Period

What you have just bought is a *tax certificate.* There is a waiting period from six months to three years (it varies from county to county) before the tax certificate can be traded in for a deed. The owner has that time to pay up the back taxes, plus 10% interest on your money. This is called the *redemption period,* and you have to sweat it out. Many owners manage to come up with the money on the very last day allowed — so the only thing you have left for all your dreams and efforts is the interest on your money.

It doesn't always work that way. I am painting it blacker than it usually is. Many properties are up for auction because the owner died and left no will or heirs (called *escheated* land). In that case, waiting out the redemption period is just a formality. There is not much chance that the owner is going to come back and reclaim the land. (At least, we have never heard of this happening.)

Buying land through county auctions is a chancy business — depending on the county. That is why we advise you to bid on several parcels if you can afford it. If you are the top bidder on three of them, with three tax certificates, you will be pretty certain to own at least one of them at the end of the redemption period. Some bidders get together with a few friends and bid on a number of properties. By playing the percentages and collecting a lot of tax certificates, each person is bound to come off with at least one parcel at the end of the redemption period.

Leftover Land

Now to answer the question: "What happens to property — land, houses, lots, etc. — that nobody bids on?" Well, if you don't write and ask about it, and nobody comes along and asks about it, it goes back on the block at the next auction. What happens if it still doesn't sell? The ownership goes back to the county. The county doesn't want it, but they are stuck with it until they can unload it at the next auction, *or by direct sale for the amount of the back taxes!* As a matter of fact, many counties are not allowed to charge more than the back taxes. The reason the county wants to unload this property is that it is just sitting there and nobody is paying taxes on it. The county can't tax itself, so they would be happy to sell it for the amount of back taxes *just to get it back on the tax rolls.*

Let's take another look at that form letter sent to county treasurers (Figure 4-1). The second sentence reads: "I am also interested in information on property which might be for sale on a Quit Claim Deed." Now you see why that sentence is in there. It refers to the property that is left over from previous county auctions — property that nobody bid on — *property that is never advertised; property that very few people know about or ever hear of* — it is *this* property that you can sometimes find and buy for $2.00 for a lot or $50.00 for a house.

Some counties have so much of this unsold property that they have a special list titled, "Properties That May Be Sold At Anytime." Many other counties have such parcels, but keep no lists. But if you show up in person at the County Treasurer's office, they will tell you what is available.

I know of a house in a small town in upstate New York that sold to the next door neighbor for $15.00. (There is a rule in some counties that leftover property must be offered to the nearest neighbor first.) You would be amazed, though, that sometimes such property is offered and the neighbor turns it down! Why? It's hard to imagine, but he could have reasons. Maybe he doesn't need any more property. Maybe he looks at it as just another building that would require upkeep, that he would have a hard time renting, and that he would have to pay taxes on. But this should not concern you, so you can grab it up without a moment's hesitation.

Another example of a stupendous bargain on leftover property is a house a friend purchased in Arlington County, Virginia. Just across the Potomac from

Washington, DC, this area is one of the richest suburbs in the United States. He bought this house for a few hundred dollars. For back taxes? No, in this case it wasn't that simple, but the story is an interesting one that we can learn something from.

Originally, the house and several others were condemned by Arlington County because they were in the path of an expressway they were planning. But before they could get started on the expressway, they changed their minds and decided not to build it. These houses were *leftovers!* After letting them sit around vacant for a few years to deteriorate, the county tore down several of them. My friend, an architect, kept going back to the courthouse and asking about this one house. They finally sold it to him. He's done some work on it since he bought it, but no major renovation was required. It was run down, but not falling apart.

Yet another example is the case of Claes-Hugo Sahlborg of Sweden. That's right — *Sweden.* Claes used the Third Edition of ***How to Buy Land Cheap*** to find a cheap house in the United States and buy it! He wrote to several counties, including Divide County, North Dakota (see the "Inside Tips" chapter), using the form letter in Figure 4-1. He ended up buying a house in Crosby, North Dakota, for $750! Figure 4-5 shows Claes standing in front of his dream house. Yes, it needs some repairs and some paint, but the house is basically sound. There is little in the way of employment opportunities in Crosby, but it doesn't bother Claes; he is retired and uses the house only 3 months out of the year. Claes bought this property from Sweden, sight unseen. Certainly if he can find cheap land from Sweden, think what's possible if you're already in the U.S.A.!

Figure 4-5

Claes-Hugo Sahlborg, a Swedish citizen, bought this house in Crosby, North Dakota, for $750 using the information in **How to Buy Land Cheap.**

Yet another example of leftover land bought using the information in this book is the case of Mr. Dennis Chilton of Springfield, Missouri. Mr. Chilton writes, "Thanks to the book *How to Buy Land Cheap,* I was able to buy a lot down by the lake for $55.14. The recording fee was $5.00 and the state 'user's fee' was $4.00, for a total cost of $64.14."

Mr. Chilton bought the land from Ozark County (see the "Inside Tips" chapter). He used our form letter and wrote to the county clerk and got back a long list of leftover property available for immediate sale on quit claim deed. He chose a nice lot on Bull Shoals Lake. He plans to build a house on the lot and sell it, probably to a senior citizen on Social Security "because of the work situation in that area." Employment may be hard to find in Ozark County, but cheap land isn't. Mr. Chilton sent us a list of leftover land still available: eight separate parcels, each under $100, were currently available!

The lesson here is that these bargains are everywhere, if you look for them... *and keep asking questions*. Keep asking the county treasurer, tax assessor and recorder if there are any leftover properties for sale. And don't overlook the county road supervisor. Sometimes he is the dark horse who *really* knows what is available. Remember, even if the answer is, "No, nothing," *county officials have been known to change their minds*.

Buying Land on Quit Claim Deeds

Suppose you have a chance to buy some of this leftover property from a county, for which you will get a Quit Claim Deed. Here are some guidelines on how to go about it. There may be variations, but this is generally the way it goes.

1. Pay the back taxes. You can do this by personal check or money order. In many cases, they are not allowed to charge you more than the back

taxes. If they do charge you more, it may only be some simple fees for paperwork.

2. The county treasurer will send you your Quit Claim Deed, and at the same time tell you that if you wish to have the sale recorded, it will be a few dollars more. Along with your check or money order, you must return the deed to the County Treasurer. (If you feel insecure about this, keep a photocopy for yourself.)

   After the deed is recorded, the County Treasurer will return your Quit Claim Deed to you. If you would like to have a map showing the exact location of your land, the treasurer will send you that, too, for a few dollars more. If this is your first land buy, you might want to frame the deed and map. They are nice to look at when city life, or your job, or something else, gets you down.

3. For future taxes, the county tax assessor will send you a long sheet with numerous personal property items listed on it which the county can tax you for. If you don't actually live on the land, this does not apply. Just write in: "I am not a resident," and return it. You won't hear anything more about this for six months, and then you will get your bill for the next year's taxes, based only on the appraised value of the land itself. *Appraised value* means what the tax assessor decides your land is worth.

Types of Deeds

Here are some definitions for common deeds. They should help you understand real estate and legal jargon when you are shopping for cheap land.

Government Patents. Signed by the President of the United States. Given to homesteaders who fulfilled the requirements.

Judgments and Decrees. These are court-issued instruments which are used in such court actions as "quiet title" judgments (see below), probate actions, and others.

Quit Claim Deed. Transfers any and all interests a seller has. Does not guarantee against future encumbrances or defects of title. The seller merely "quits his claim" to the property.

Warranty Deeds. A warranty deed assures that the title is free and clear of encumbrances, defects and liens, and can be sued upon if it is breached.

Tax Deeds. Issued to those who purchase property for back taxes. In order to be marketable, tax titles usually require a "quiet title action." The quiet title action is simply a suit brought against all persons, known or unknown, who might have an interest in or claim to a piece of property. If no one turns up at the action with a better claim, the court issues a decree granting clear title, as a judgment against these parties.

- 5 -
BUYING LAND CHEAP
FROM
THE FEDERAL GOVERNMENT

How do you get land directly from the federal government? There is still plenty of U.S. Government land to get — millions of acres — but it has to be approached through the right channels. Which brings up one of the important points of this book, and that is: *with rare exceptions, none of this land or property is widely advertised for sale. It is not even publicized that such lands exist and might be for sale.* But it is, if you know where to apply. Yes, you can buy land from the federal government. The quickest way to find a small tract is to read the listings in the *Federal Register* (available in many libraries).

The Bureau of Land Management

The best way to find out about current federal government policies on the sale of land is to write to the U.S. Department of the Interior, Bureau of Land Management, Washington, DC 20240, and ask for the pamphlet, "Are There Any Public Lands for Sale?" Because land sale programs change from time to time, this pamphlet will keep you up to date and answer common questions. For more direct results, though, you can follow the instructions given here.

The Bureau of Land Management (BLM) handles the sale of *most* federally owned lands. The national office of the BLM used to keep a record of all BLM land for sale anywhere, and publish a listing in a magazine called *Our Public Lands*. Now, they no longer keep any such listing, and *Our Public Lands* is just a feature magazine of articles on land use policies. While Congress has set the guidelines for the sale of public land, control over auctions of BLM lands has been turned over to BLM regional offices.

While the BLM owns millions of acres of land, they are stingy about selling it off. Land to be sold must first meet the following criteria:

1. The government doesn't need the land (that includes state and local governments, who must be offered the land first).
2. The land must be uneconomical to manage (scattered, isolated tracts with no apparent value).
3. The reasons the lands were acquired are no longer in force.
4. Sale of the land serves a public objective.

Basically, what all this means is that the federal government doesn't want to part with land unless it has to. When it has land it doesn't really want, it usually tries to swap it for land it does want. When land is offered for sale, there is preference given to neighboring property owners. Finally, when they do sell the land to the general public, they usually reserve mineral rights and any other easements they think might come in handy some day.

So if you think there's no land available from the BLM, you're only half right. There's still a chance to get in on some very good deals, before Congress shuts the land buying window altogether. The way things are going, the federal government is never going to sell land — just play landlord, or swap unwanted land for other land it wants. But right now, some regional BLMs sell off *a lot* of land. If you are discouraged because the ones you write to don't have land for sale, then broaden your horizons. The BLM in Nevada sells *thousands of acres* of land every few months, and it's not just desert, either. Much of the land is prime residential subdivision property (and some of the bids are quite high). Figure 5-1 shows a page of the bid results from the August 15, 1990, BLM of Nevada sale. While the parcels of land aren't described except as to size, the chart gives you some idea of the value of these lands and how the bidding goes.

In our recent survey of BLM offices, we found that most had no land for sale, some keep mailing lists and some do not. A few of the western offices had land for sale, and some of the prices were quite good ($50 parcels in Oregon, Wyoming and Nevada, for example). Many of the offices sent beautiful maps. Others were much less helpful. If you're interested in land in a certain area, and the BLM doesn't have anything, you'll have to try other sources. But if you don't care where your cheap land is located, you can find some at rock-bottom prices from the BLM.

Because everything is done on the regional level, you'll have to do a little more work if you want to find out about land sales in different states. Each BLM regional office sets its own policies regarding the sale of lands. All of them require that the purchaser be a U.S. citizen or corporation, but they differ as to whether sales are by auction or sealed bid, the amount of deposit required for bidding, and how quickly the balance must be paid by successful bidders.

You can get information on the lands available for sale and the methods for conducting sales from each BLM regional office as listed below. I recommend that you use a form letter like the one in Figure 5-2 if you're going to contact more than a couple of these offices. This should get you the kind of accurate information you need to get to the next step: bidding on a piece of land.

RESULTS OF THE AUGUST 15, 1990
BID OPENING

Parcel No.	Serial No.	Acreage	Appraised Value	Successful Bidder	Address	Sale Price	Bid Deposit
81-01	N-33501	2.50	$ 66,300	Jay N. Smith	8240 Hickam Ave, LV, NV 89129	92,215.00	13,832.25
81-02	N-33502	2.50	65,000	Robert T. Mendenhall	1701 Duneville, LV, NV 89102	85,020.00	12,753.00
81-03	N-33503	2.50	65,000	C. Ronald & Patsy J. Eggert	4008 Meadow Valley Ct., LV, NV 89107//3175 Montessouri St. LV, NV 89117	90,150.00	13,522.50
81-04	N-33504	2.50	68,400	Dieter B. & Ann Lehner, APL Properties, Inc.	2810 W. Charleston, G-67 LV, NV 89102	81,100.00	12,165.00
81-05	N-33505	2.50	62,900	Fee H. & Rosa M. Ong	2997 Harbor Cove Dr. LV, NV 89128	82,500.00	12,375.00
81-07	N-33507	5.00	89,700	Jeffery B. Kinner, DDS / Anne M. Kinner	5817 Martita Ave. LV, NV 89108	126,600.00	20,000.00
81-09	N-33509	5.00	160,000	Jeffery B. Kinner, DDS / Anne M. Kinner	5817 Martita Ave. LV, NV 89108	191,000.00	30,000.00
81-11	N-33511	2.50	63,100	Luther Kutcher	4720 Tomsik LV, NV 89129	77,000.00	11,600.00
81-12	N-33512	2.50	63,800	R. M. Tiberti	500 S. Third, No. 3, LV, NV 89101	74,130.00	11,119.50
81-13	N-33513	2.50	54,000	Valleywide Realty & Investments	3149 Clamdigger Lane LV, NV 89117	68,100.00	10,215.00
81-14	N-33514	2.50	51,800	Jozef Havaldo / Rick Iknoian	3508 Corona Del Mar Las Vegas, NV 89108	68,170.00	10,225.50
81-15	N-33515	15.00	303,000	Ron C. Ayers	P. O. Box 81260 LV, NV 89180	546,000.00	81,900.00
81-16	N-33516	2.50	63,100	R. M. Tiberti	500 S. Third, No. 3, LV, NV 89101	64,110.00	9,620.00
81-17	N-33517	5.00	112,800	Valley Bank of Nevada; Trustee, El Cortez Profit Sharing Plan	Box 98555, LV, NV 89193	136,006.67	20,401.00
81-18	N-33518	5.00	115,200	Dr. & Mrs. Scott A. Slavis//Mrs. Mindy G. Salvis	2813 High Sail Court LV, NV 89117	117,220.00	17,590.00
81-19	N-33519	5.00	88,500	Valley Bank of Nevada; Trustee, El Cortez Profit Sharing Plan — NO HIGH BIDDER DECLARED--ONLY BID RECEIVED WAS INVALID	Box 98555, LV, NV 89193		
81-21	N-33521	10.00	178,000	Albert Abrams Family Trust//Albert Abrams, Trustee	5300 W. Sahara Ave. No. 201, LV, NV 89102	211,900.00	31,785.00

Figure 5-1

*A page of bid results from a
Las Vegas, Nevada, BLM auction.*

Your Name
Your Street Address
Your City, State, Zip Code

Date

Bureau of Land Management
Regional Office Address
City, State, Zip Code

Dear Sir or Madam,

I am interested in purchasing land from the federal government. Could you please send me notification of any BLM auctions in your jurisdiction, along with descriptions of the property for sale, bid applications, and rules and regulations concerning bidding procedures?

I would also like to have my name placed on your mailing list for notification of future land sales.

Thank you for your assistance.

Sincerely,

(Signature)

Figure 5-2

A sample form letter to use when writing to Bureau of Land Management regional offices.

Bidding on BLM Land

This is where the going gets tricky. While the sale of BLM land is technically administered by BLM *regional offices*, the actual sales are conducted by BLM *district offices* (subdivisions of regional offices). If you want to bid on a piece of land, you write to a *district office* to get a description of the land, the date of the sale, and the application and bid forms.

Sale of BLM land is typically handled this way: When the regional BLM determines that pieces of land are excess to its needs, it initiates the sales process. Land is offered for sale using one of the following three methods: competitive bids (with preferences for nearby landowners), competitive public bids, or non-competitive direct sales. The competitive public bids can be either by mail (sealed bids) or by oral auction. In either case, you do not have to be present to bid (in the case of oral bids, you can send a representative).

Bids that are mailed must be accompanied by a deposit, usually equal to some fraction of the minimum bid (say, 10%). The land goes to the highest bidder. In most cases, the land must be paid for in full, immediately. Sometimes, the federal government will give an extension on financing, if the high bidder is a non-profit organization and the land is intended for "public" use. But the BLM does not provide any long-term financing for sales. Deposits are promptly returned to the losing bidders.

None of the land offered for sale by the BLM has obvious agricultural uses. Such lands are offered for private sales to potential users, as are lands with suspected mineral values. In other words, oil companies and farmers get to bid privately on lands they can use. The lands open to competitive public bidding do not have productive values (usually). Most of this land is isolated desert land or near-wilderness. Still, you may find just the Shangri-La you've been looking for.

You should be careful when you bid on this land to be sure you have access to the land or a right of way easement so you can get to it. Also, in many cases the federal government will retain all title to the mineral rights on the land. If you find oil or natural gas, it's theirs, not yours.

BLM Offices

Here are the addresses and phone numbers for the BLM Regional Offices, followed by the District Office addresses for each region:

ALASKA:
Regional Office:
Bureau of Land Management
701 "C" St, Box 13
Anchorage, AK 99513
(907) 271-5555

Anchorage District Office:
Bureau of Land Management
4700 E 72 Ave
Anchorage, AK 99507

Fairbanks District Office:
Bureau of Land Management
PO Box 3505
Fort Wainwright, AK 99703

ARIZONA:
Regional Office:
3707 N 7th St
Phoenix, AZ 85011
(602) 261-3821

Arizona Strip District Office:
Bureau of Land Management
390 N 3050 St
St. George, UT 84770

Phoenix District Office:
Bureau of Land Management
2015 W Deer Valley Rd
Phoenix, AZ 85027

Safford District Office:
Bureau of Land Management
425 E Fourth St
Safford, AZ 85546

CALIFORNIA:
Regional Office:
Bureau of Land Management
2800 Cottage Way
Sacramento, CA 95825
(916) 978-4720

Bakersfield District Office:
Bureau of Land Management
800 Trustun Ave, Rm 311
Bakersfield, CA 93301

California Desert District Office:
Bureau of Land Management
1695 Spruce St
Riverside, CA 92507

Susanville District Office:
Bureau of Land Management
PO Box 1090
Centerville Rd
Susanville, CA 96130

Ukiah District Office:
Bureau of Land Management
555 Leslie St
Ukiah, CA 95482

COLORADO (includes Kansas):
Regional Office:
Bureau of Land Management
2850 Youngfield St
Lakewood, CO 80215
(303) 236-1756

Canon City District Office:
Bureau of Land Management
3080 E Main St
PO Box 311
Canon City, CO 81212

Craig District Office:
Bureau of Land Management
455 Emerson St
Craig, CO 81625

Grand Junction District Office:
Bureau of Land Management
764 Horizon Dr
Grand Junction, CO 81401

IDAHO:
Regional Office:
Bureau of Land Management
3380 Americana Terrace
Boise, ID 83706
(202) 334-1770

Boise District Office:
Bureau of Land Management
3948 Development Ave
Boise, ID 83705

Burley District Office:
Bureau of Land Management
Route 3, Box 1
200 S Oakley Hwy
Burley, ID 83318

Coeur d'Alene District Office:
Bureau of Land Management
1808 N Third St
Coeur d'Alene, ID 83814

Idaho Falls District Office:
Bureau of Land Management
940 Lincoln Rd
Idaho Falls, ID 83401

Salmon District Office:
Bureau of Land Management
PO Box 430
Salmon, ID 83467

Shoshone District Office:
Bureau of Land Management
PO Box 2-B
400 West F St
Shoshone, ID 83352

MONTANA (including North and South Dakota):
Regional Office:
Bureau of Land Management
222 N 32 St
PO Box 36800
Billings, MT 59107
(406) 255-2913

Butte District Office:
Bureau of Land Management
106 N Parkmont
PO Box 3388
Butte, MT 59702

Dickinson District Office:
Bureau of Land Management
2933 Third Ave W
Dickinson, ND 58601

Lewiston District Office:
Bureau of Land Management
Airport Road
PO Box 1160
Lewiston, MT 59457

Miles City District Office:
Bureau of Land Management
Garyowen Road
PO Box 940
Miles City, MT 59301

NEVADA:
Regional Office:
Bureau of Land Management
830 Harvard Way
PO Box 12000
Reno, NV 89520
(702) 785-6500

Battle Mountain District Office:
Bureau of Land Management
N 2nd & Scott Sts
PO Box 1420
Battle Mountain, NV 89820

Elko District Office:
Bureau of Land Management
3900 E Idaho St
PO Box 831
Elko, NV 89801

Ely District Office:
Bureau of Land Management
Star Rte 5, Box 1
Ely, NV 89301

Las Vegas District Office:
Bureau of Land Management
PO Box 26569
4765 W Vegas Dr
Las Vegas, NV 89126

Winnemucca District Office:
Bureau of Land Management
705 E Fourth St
Winnemucca, NV 89445

NEW MEXICO (includes Oklahoma and Texas):
Regional Office:
Bureau of Land Management
Montoya Federal Bldg
PO Box 1449
Santa Fe, NM 87501
(505) 988-6316

Las Cruces District Office:
Bureau of Land Management
317 N Main
PO Box 1420
Las Cruces, NM 88004

Roswell District Office:
Bureau of Land Management
1717 W Second St
PO Box 1397
Roswell, NM 88201

OREGON (includes Washington):
Regional Office:
Bureau of Land Management
825 NE Multnomah St
PO Box 2965
Portland, OR 97208
(503) 231-6277

North Bend District Office:
Bureau of Land Management
1300 Airport Lane
North Bend, OR 97459

Eugene District Office:
Bureau of Land Management
1255 Peral St
PO Box 10226
Eugene, OR 97401

Lakeview District Office:
Bureau of Land Management
1000 Ninth St S
PO Box 151
Lakeview, OR 97630

Medford District Office:
Bureau of Land Management
3040 Biddle Rd
Medford, OR 97405

Prineville District Office:
Bureau of Land Management
185 E Fourth St
PO Box 550
Prineville, OR 97754

Roseburg District Office:
Bureau of Land Management
777 NW Garden Valley Blvd
Roseburg, OR 97470

Salem District Office:
Bureau of Land Management
1717 Fabry Rd SE
PO Box 3227
Salem, OR 97302

Spokane District Office:
Bureau of Land Management
E 4217 Main
Spokane, WA 99202

Vale District Office:
Bureau of Land Management
100 Oregon St
Vale, OR 97918

UTAH:
Regional Office:
Bureau of Land Management
324 S State St, #301
PO Box 45155
Salt Lake City, UT 84145
(801) 539-4001

Cedar City District Office:
Bureau of Land Management
PO Box 724
Cedar City, UT 84720

Moab District Office:
Bureau of Land Management
PO Box 970
Moab, UT 84532

Richfield District Office:
Bureau of Land Management
150 E 900 North
Richfield, UT 84701

Salt Lake City District Office:
Bureau of Land Management
2370 S 2300 West
Salt Lake City, UT 84119

Vernal District Office:
Bureau of Land Management
170 S 500 East
Vernal, UT 84078

WYOMING (including Nebraska):
Regional Office:
Bureau of Land Management
2515 Warren Ave
PO Box 1828
Cheyenne, WY 82003
(307) 775-6256

Casper District Office:
Bureau of Land Management
951 Rancho Rd
Casper, WY 82601

Rawlins District Office:
Bureau of Land Management
1300 Third St
Rawlins, WY 82301

Rock Springs District Office:
Bureau of Land Management
PO Box 1869
Highway 191 N
Rock Springs, WY 82901

Worland District Office:
Bureau of Land Management
PO Box 119
1700 Robertson Ave
Worland, WY 82401

EASTERN STATES OFFICE (including all other states):
Regional Office:
Bureau of Land Management
350 S Pickett St
Alexandria, VA 22304
(703) 461-1328

Northern District Office:
Bureau of Land Management
310 W Wisconsin Ave
Milwaukee, WI 53203

The Savings & Loan Crisis

Probably the biggest cheap land bonanza to come along since homesteading is a result of the Savings and Loan crisis of the 1980s. Savings and Loan Associations (S&Ls) started going bankrupt by the dozen after the collapse of the sunbelt economy in the early 1980s. Congress formed the Resolution Trust Corporation (RTC) to mop up the S&L mess. As S&Ls are declared bankrupt, their marketable assets are transferred to healthier banks. The junk nobody wants is transferred to the RTC to dispose of.

The RTC sells just about every kind of land or structure: houses, apartment buildings, condominiums, commercial buildings, mobile homes, building lots, agricultural land, mining properties, etc. Prices range from a couple hundred bucks to millions of dollars per piece. By law, the RTC is required to sell everything at "fair market value." As we've seen, "fair market value" can be dirt cheap. And those parcels that can't be sold for the RTC's estimate of fair market value will be auctioned off.

Getting RTC Listings

Even though the RTC is part of the federal government, there is no way of getting a free listing of the properties they sell. Listings are put together in large books the RTC calls *Real Estate Asset Inventories*. The listing for commercial property is $25.00. The other listings, shown below, are $15.00 each. You might try getting a copy from your local library before buying a list:

- Single Family Residences in Texas
- Single Family Residences Everywhere Else
- Multi-Family Residences
- Condominiums, Mobile Homes and Residential Lots
- Land

You can buy the listings over the phone using a major credit card. The toll free number is 1-800-RTC-3006. Don't try to get any other information over the phone — I tried several times, and it was useless. This is a program run by the federal government; it is slow, unresponsive and annoying. You can also purchase the listings by mail. Send check or money order and a description of the guides you want to:

Resolution Trust Corporation
Real Estate Excess Inventory
PO Box 539002
Grand Prairie, TX 75053.

Once you have ordered, prepare for a long wait. It took over a month for my listings to get to me.

The land list is about the size of a small phone book. It has over 180 pages of listings with over 35,000 properties for sale. The address for each property is given, along with the size, zoning, list price and contact name. A lot of the listings are out of date. Of 14 properties I called about, 12 had been sold before the list was even put together and the other two had sales pending. There are some exceptional bargains, but it may take patience to find them.

As you might have guessed, most of the listings are in Texas. If you are thinking of relocating to Texas, this is the way to go. There are also ample listings for other sunbelt states. The pickings are kind of slim when it comes to the east coast, the midwest and the northwest.

Buying the Properties

If you have found a listing that interests you, the next step is to make contact with the sales agent. A broker is listed for each property. In most cases, a local broker handles the sale on behalf of the RTC. So you won't be calling the RTC, or one of its agents, to buy the property; you'll be contacting a local real estate agent.

The local real estate agents are empowered to cut any deal they can, so long as they get 95% of "fair market value" (FMV). The FMV is set by an appraisal made by an RTC appraisor. You'll notice that most of the land for sale does not have a list price. The RTC doesn't bother to get an appraisal until someone shows an interest in the property. So you may have to wait for an appraisal before the local real estate broker can start dealing with you. Just like every transaction with the RTC, you should be prepared for a good long wait. It could be months before they get around to appraising the piece you're interested in.

Once you have a list price, you can start to deal. Of course, you probably won't offer any more than the list price. If you think the list price is too high, you can put in any bid you want. If the broker wants to get rid of the property, they may have to ask for a re-appraisal to sell it to you for the lower price. That's right — you could be waiting months for the RTC to complete a new appraisal.

If you come to terms on price, then the deal can be closed fairly quickly. All RTC properties are sold "as is," so it's up to you to inspect the property and verify that it is what they say it is. There are no guarantees as to title, either. You will have to perform a Quiet Title action (see the Glossary) to secure good title to the property.

The RTC says they will have an auction for all those properties where no one in the market is interested at the "fair market value." However, this auction has been

postponed several times, and you cannot trust anything they say about setting a date. The best you can
hope for is to stay in touch with the RTC and maybe
you'll find out about the auction before it happens (if
it happens).

The General Services Administration

Another source for inexpensive property from the
federal government is the General Services Administration (GSA). This agency doesn't sell much undeve-
loped land; it usually sells improved property including
buildings that are no longer of use to the government.
All federal agencies are required to notify the GSA
whenever they have property they no longer have a use
for. The GSA then sees if any other agency has a use
for it. If no one wants it (not even the states), then it
goes on the auction block.

The GSA publishes a bi-monthly listing of all the
properties they currently have for sale. It's called the
U.S. Real Property Sales List, and is available free of
charge from:

Consumer Information Center
Pueblo, CO 81009.

The Consumer Information Center does not keep a
mailing list, so you must write for it every two months.

Properties are arranged in the Sales List by regional
sales offices. The regional offices do not keep mailing
lists either. You must send in an Application for Notice
of Individual Sales like the one shown in Figure 5-3.
Each time a sale is conducted, you will receive notice

and an application for notice of the next sale. Listings are also advertised in the *Commerce Business Daily*, which is available by subscription from:

> Superintendent of Documents
> U.S. Government Printing Office
> Washington, DC 20402.

Commerce Business Daily is basically a newspaper for contractors doing business with the government, or for those who wish they were. Only a small portion of the newspaper deals with government property for sale, and you can find this information for less money elsewhere. Subscriptions to *Commerce Business Daily* run $261.00 per year. Single issues are not available.

A better way to go is to write to the GSA Sales Offices that cover the areas you're interested in at the addresses given below. When you receive notification of a property sale that sounds interesting, write them again and request an *Invitation for Bid*. They will send you a description of the property, the terms and conditions of sale, and complete bidding instructions.

The kind of stuff they sell varies greatly. I would say that more than half of it is military forts or training centers. Many of the listings include more than 20 buildings on a single site, so they're not going to be *inexpensive* (though they may be *cheap*). There are also warehouses, grain elevators, Post Offices and old federal buildings. Considering that every single federal agency has a chance to pick up these gems for only the cost of maintenance, I suspect that they're less than desirable properties. But beauty is in the eye of the beholder, right?

How To Obtain Issues
of the U.S. Real Property Sales List

GSA does not maintain a mailing list for future issues of the
U.S. Real Property Sales List.

If you would like to receive the next edition, complete this
order blank and mail it to the address indicated. You will need to
send in the order blank from each issue you receive in order to
receive the following issue.

Please use correct postage.

How To Obtain Notices of Individual Sales

If you would like to receive notices of individual sales of U.S.
Government real property, complete this form and detach and mail
it to us. Your name will be placed on a permanent mailing list for
the locations you indicate. Unlike the one above, you need to
complete this form only once. Your name and address will remain
on the list until such time as we ask you to validate the information.

For the **Location** section of the card, you may select up to
three states or territories. Write the four-digit numbers of the
locations (from the list below) into the boxes. Please print clearly.

0001-AL	0019-IA	0033-NH	0048-TX
0002-AK	0020-KS	0034-NJ	0049-UT
0004-AZ	0021-KY	0035-NM	0050-VT
0005-AR	0022-LA	0036-NY	0051-VA
0006-CA	0023-ME	0037-NC	0053-WA
0008-CO	0024-MD	0038-ND	0054-WV
0009-CT	0025-MA	0039-OH	0055-WI
0010-DE	0026-MI	0040-OK	0056-WY
0012-FL	0027-MN	0041-OR	0057-Am. Samoa
0013-GA	0028-MS	0042-PA	0011-DC
0015-HI	0029-MO	0044-RI	0058-Guam
0016-ID	0030-MT	0045-SC	0043-PR
0017-IL	0031-NE	0046-SD	0059-Pac. Is. Ter.
0018-IN	0032-NV	0047-TN	0052-VI

If you are interested in all types of real property located
anywhere in the 50 states and/or the District of Columbia, Puerto
Rico, the U.S. Virgin Islands, American Samoa, Guam, or the U.S.
Pacific trust territories, check the box under **All Locations and
Types**. You will then receive all notices issued by all of GSA's
regional real estate sales offices.

Issues of the U.S. Real Property Sales List   **E**

Mail to: Properties — E, Consumer Information Center
          Pueblo, CO 81009

Please send the next issue of the **U.S. Real Property
Sales List** to (type or print in ink):

_____
NAME

_____
STREET

_____
CITY   STATE (TWO-LETTER MAIL CODE)   ZIP

- -

Notices of Individual Sales

Mail to: U.S. General Services Administration (9KS)
         525 Market Street
         San Francisco, CA 94105

If you could like to receive notices of individual sales of Federal real
property, complete the appropriate items and mail this form to the
address above.

Type of Property (Check one or more boxes)

☐ Agriculture, timber, grazing,   ☐ Industrial
  and minerals

☐ Commercial   ☐ Residential

Location of Property (Write in the four-digit numbers from the list
opposite of the locations for which you wish to receive sales
notices.)

☐☐☐☐ Location ☐☐☐☐ Location ☐☐☐☐ Location
☐ *All locations and types*

Name and Address for Notices (Please print clearly with one letter
or number per box.)

☐☐☐☐☐☐☐☐☐☐☐☐☐☐☐☐☐☐☐☐☐☐☐
NAME

☐☐☐☐☐☐☐☐☐☐☐☐☐☐☐☐☐   ☐☐☐☐
STREET   APT. OR SUITE

☐☐☐☐☐☐☐☐☐☐☐☐☐   ☐☐   ☐☐☐☐☐
CITY   STATE   ZIP

Figure 5-3

Application for notice of GSA sales (with instructions).

And then there are the gems. Remember, finding cheap land is a matter of persistence. And persistence brought us notice of an amazing opportunity from the GSA in Auburn, Washington. The Auburn GSA was trying to get rid of the Celilo Ranch in Rufus, Oregon. The "ranch" is 168 acres, has its own spring for water and is hooked up to city water, sewer, telephone and other amenities. It is located on the Columbia River near Mt. Hood and is just 20 minutes from The Dalles, Oregon, which is becoming one of the windsurfing capitals of the world. The ranch is not isolated (it is in the town of Rufus, population 350) and it is not barren. The price? $50,000 — just $300 an acre.

The Celilo Ranch is not dirt cheap; you can't buy it for a day's wages (unless you are one wealthy dude). But it is an exceptional bargain, the kind of thing that will pay off handsomely for the investor who has plenty of cash and plenty of time. This ranch could be the perfect retreat, a place to spend weekends (90 minutes from Portland, Oregon) and vacations while preparing to subdivide the property into home sites (the spring water can support up to 20 homes). A map of the Celilo Ranch is shown in Figure 5-4. We just learned that the ranch sold at auction for $61,610. While the Celilo Ranch is no longer available, it illustrates the importance of building up a little nest egg to be able to take advantage of the exceptional opportunities that are going to come your way when you follow the advice in this book.

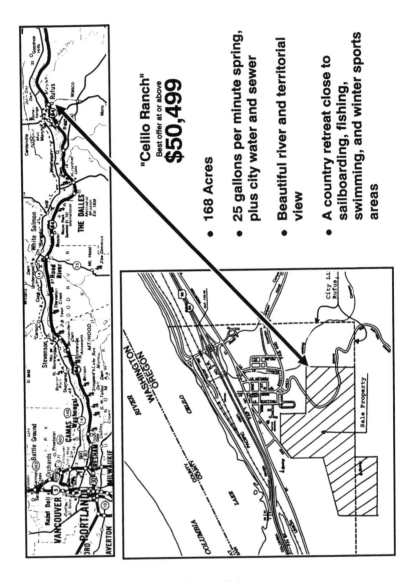

"Celilo Ranch"
Best offer at or above
$50,499

- 168 Acres
- 25 gallons per minute spring, plus city water and sewer
- Beautiful river and territorial view
- A country retreat close to sailboarding, fishing, swimming, and winter sports areas

Figure 5-4

Sale announcement by the Auburn, Washington, GSA for the Celilo Ranch in Rufus, Oregon.

All GSA sales are for CASH. Most sales are by competitive sealed bids. A deposit of 10% of the minimum bid is required when you send in your offer. The property is awarded to the highest bidder, though the award process takes as much as 60 days. Deposits are promptly returned to unsuccessful bidders.

GSA Sales Offices

For New York, New Jersey, Connecticut, Rhode Island, Massachusetts, Vermont, New Hampshire, Maine, Ohio, Indiana, Michigan, Illinois, Wisconsin, Minnesota, Puerto Rico and Virgin Islands:

Office of Real Estate Sales (2DR-1)
U.S. General Services Administration
10 Causeway St
Boston, MA 02222
(617) 565-5700

For Pennsylvania, Delaware, Maryland, District of Columbia, Virginia, West Virginia, Kentucky, Tennessee, North Carolina, South Carolina, Mississippi, Alabama, Georgia and Florida:

Office of Real Estate Sales (4DR)
U.S. General Services Administration
75 Spring St SW, Room 818
Atlanta, GA 30303
(404) 331-5133

For Montana, North Dakota, South Dakota, Wyoming, Nebraska, Iowa, Missouri, Arkansas, Louisiana,

Texas, Oklahoma, New Mexico, Kansas, Colorado and Utah:

> Office of Real Estate Sales (7DR)
> U.S. General Services Administration
> 819 Taylor St, Room 11A26
> Fort Worth, TX 76102
> (817) 334-2331

For Arizona, California, Nevada, Idaho, Oregon, Washington, Alaska, Hawaii and Guam:

> Office of Real Estate Sales (9DR)
> U.S. General Services Administration
> 525 Market St
> San Francisco, CA 94105
> (415) 744-5952

Other Sources of Cheap Federal Land

As I've stressed throughout this book, you can find cheap land if you just *keep looking!* There are pockets of land being held in dozens of federal, state and county agencies. The more you dig, the more you find. *And it's when you uncover these forgotten parcels that you get the land at rock-bottom prices!* So let's look at some other places where we might find land in the federal bureaucracy.

Farmers Home Administration

The Department of Agriculture's Farmers Home Administration (FmHA) occasionally disposes of properties it acquires through mortgage foreclosures. Most of these are small farms — just the perfect thing for inexpensive land hunters looking to get out of the big city! For information on these lands, contact the County Supervisor, Farmers Home Administration, in the counties where you are interested in buying land. Most of these offices are located in the county seat.

Health and Human Services

The Department of Health and Human Services (formerly Health, Education and Welfare) offers properties for sale for next to nothing to non-profit organizations that agree to use them for approved "health" purposes. They offer a 30 year free lease, and at the end of that period, if the organization has not violated the terms of the lease, title is transferred to the non-profit organization. For more information, contact:

Director of Office of Real Property
Department of Health and Human Services
Washington, DC 20201

Department of Education

The Department of Education runs a program similar to the Health and Human Services program above. It would not be surprising to find several other federal agencies selling off small parcels of land. The number of such sales are so few that this would hardly be considered one of your main sources. Still, if you're determined to find land in a specific area, and you haven't turned up anything with the other methods in this book, you can keep writing to government agencies and sooner or later you're going to knock something loose. *Maybe it'll be the dream place you've always wanted!*

Small Business Administration

The liquidation division of the Small Business Administration also sells property. Contact the office nearest to your desired location, as there is no information on this at the national level.

Internal Revenue Service

Cheap land and other property can also be bought from the Internal Revenue Service (IRS). When people owe the IRS tax money, and haven't responded to requests for payment, the IRS can and does confiscate their property to sell in order to get the taxes owed them. The IRS is legally required to give public notice of all such sales, unless perishable goods are involved. Notice is sent to people on their mailing list, and the sale is announced in the common newspaper of the county of sale.

You can get your name on the IRS auction mailing list by writing or calling the IRS office in the county of interest. Some of the decisions regarding the method of sale are made by the IRS Revenue Office in charge of the sale. Sales may be by sealed (mailed) bids, or by public auctions. The sale is always held in the county where the property was seized. Public auctions are usually held at IRS headquarters in that county.

IRS auctions are usually good bargains because they want to sell the property *fast*. When they seize property, they estimate its value, and then discount that to a "forced-sale value," that is, the price it would bring if sold under duress. They then deduct all mortgages or other encumbrances from the forced-sale value to arrive at the minimum acceptable bid. It should be noted, though, that they don't do a title search in most cases, and there may be more claims against the property than they know of.

You should be warned that when you buy property from the IRS, you do not have title free and clear. You must still settle any outstanding claims against the property. The IRS does not make any guarantees as to the amount of claims against the property, though they will tell you all they know. You may want to do a title search yourself before you bid.

Bids mailed in must be accompanied by a deposit equal to 20% of your bid (not the minimum bid) or $200, whichever is less. Property sold at public auctions must be paid for in full in cash, cashiers check or money order, within 24 hours. The former owner has a 180-day redemption period in which to buy back the property. But he or she must pay 20% interest on your money. For more information on IRS sales, contact your county IRS office and ask to be placed on their auction mailing list.

Drug Enforcement Administration

The U.S. Department of Justice Drug Enforcement Administration (DEA) also confiscates property involved in criminal activity. In most cases, they turn the property over to the GSA to sell for them, but there are exceptions. Check with your nearest DEA office to find out the policy in your area.

- 6 -
BUYING LAND CHEAP FROM STATE GOVERNMENTS

Suppose you haven't found your dream place yet after poring through atlases and farm catalogs and writing a few dozen letters to county and federal bureaucrats. Where do you go next? Are there other places to hunt for cheap land?

YOU BET! There's still state land, city land, and land in foreign countries! An amazing amount of land changes hands every day. If you haven't found anything yet, there are still other sources to check. By the time you've checked most of them, you can go back and double-check with the most likely sources. If they didn't have anything six months ago, they may have just what you're after *now!*

Availability of State Lands

Lands owned by the states were originally given to them by the federal government to help them meet the costs of public education. The states now buy and sell land on a regular basis, and manage these lands for the highest profit. If you can't buy your favorite piece of land, you may be able to get a long-term lease on it, or just rights to live on it for a stated period of time.

Most of the state land up for sale is in the Western states. The federal government owns about 75% of all the land west of the Mississippi, and the states own as much as 10%. Much of this government land is leased out to ranchers for grazing, but there are still large tracts of 40 acres and up that can be bought at auction from time to time.

Land availability in the eastern U.S. is a little tighter, and when you find it, it usually isn't "cheap." But there are bargains around. In the states east of the Mississippi, you'll have to do a little more digging to unearth the earth you're after. But the result could be a choice piece of land that nobody knew existed. And the price could be surprisingly cheap!

A good example of cheap land in the east is the State of Maine. At their 1990 sale of tax acquired property, the following parcel was available for a minimum bid of $50.00: "A 1.04 acre lot near U.S. Route 2. The site was formerly occupied by a camp which has fallen down. The site is growing to hardwood." Sounds kind of nice, doesn't it? The same auction offered a 60 acre parcel with a collapsed house on it for $440.00. That's about $7.50 an acre!

Finding State Lands

There are two main sources for information on land for sale from the states: the State Land Commissioner and the State Highway Commissioner. Send off a letter to both of them in care of the state capitol, as shown in Figure 6-1. Ask them if they have any "surplus" land for sale, and mention several specific categories: Tax foreclosed land, unused government properties, abandoned estates, leftover highway land, unused school properties, etc. If you just tell them "surplus lands," they may tell you they have none. For some reason these folks don't like the word "surplus." It makes it sound like they have more resources than they need, and they might be afraid of getting their budget cut if someone finds out. So be sure to specify the kind of land you're looking for.

Another word of caution is to NOT ask for "cheap land." If you do, they will respond something like this: "All properties are appraised and sold at fair market value. There are no 'cheap' lands available in our state." They don't want the taxpayers to think they're selling off the homeland for less than it's worth. Of course, market value could be *very cheap* — especially if no one knows the land even exists. If you ask for "cheap land," they'll send you the above statement and no listings of land. So humor them and ask for surplus lands, and explain what you mean. You don't want to have to write to them twice just to get the basic information.

Many state agencies keep mailing lists for announcing land sales and auctions. You can be put on these lists for free or for some minimal charge. Other states send out lists with descriptions of the actual parcels up for sale, and these lists usually cost a couple of bucks. If you've narrowed your land search down to a manageable area, it will save you time and aggravation if you're on the mailing list.

Your Name
Your Street Address
Your City, State, Zip Code

Date

Commissioner of Lands
State Capitol
City, State, Zip Code

Dear Sir or Madam,

Please send me information about real estate in your jurisdiction which might be auctioned off or available for private sale.

This might include tax foreclosed property, unused government property, abandoned estates, or any other land that might be surplus to your needs.

If you keep a mailing list for notification of real estate auctions or sales, would you please add my name or send me an application for adding my name to the list?

Thank you for your assistance.

Sincerely,

(Signature)

Figure 6-1

A sample form letter to use when writing to state governments in search of cheap land.

As we said, the simplest way to get information on state land is to write to the State Land Commissioner and the State Highway Commissioner. If you don't get a positive response from them, DON'T GIVE UP! *There are many other agencies that sell or auction land in the states. With enough persistence, you are bound to stumble on something you like.*

For example, most states have a Department of Natural Resources (DNR) which manages large tracts of state lands. There are also Departments of Parks & Recreation, Game, Forestry, Fisheries & Wildlife, etc. These departments often buy up land for state management, decide they no longer need it, and sell it off again. State Departments of Transportation, Water Resources, Sewage and Bridges also sell parcels of land.

You can write to these departments in care of the state capitol in the capital city of the state you're interested in. In many cases, you won't have the exactly correct department title or address, but don't worry — your letters will get forwarded. These little known sources of land are well worth the effort of checking. When you find something, you're likely to get it at a bargain price!

The harder you look, the more state agencies you will find that sell land. It might be worth a couple of dollars to buy a directory of state government in the states you're looking at. Even the most unlikely agencies may have land to dispose of.

Did you know that most state universities are sellers of land? They're given land by the state or private groups or individuals which they sell off according to their financial needs. There are also state agencies that handle the sale of escheated lands (owner died with no heir or will), though these are more often handled on the county or city level.

So you see, if you don't get immediate satisfaction from the major land sellers of the state, and you are determined to find land, you have many alternative sources to go to. Below are some specific addresses for places you might be interested in. They should give you some ideas for similar departments to check out in your chosen states.

Mineral Rights

There is a warning when buying land cheap from the states. Not bad news, just something to watch out for: almost always when land is sold by the state, *the state keeps all the mineral rights*. Think about this and ask yourself just what it could mean. Suppose you find gold in your creek. Or suppose you dig a well and the water is all black and oily. The gold and the oil belong to the state! If these things mean anything to you, check this out before you buy.

Now let's look at some of the better places for finding cheap state land.

Alaska
The state of Alaska probably auctions off, or *gives away*, more land than any other state. It seems to be one of the only places that actively seeks out people to give land to. Programs are changing all the time, but

here's some current information on how to get cheap land in Alaska.

In 1984, Alaska began a new homesteading program. To participate, you must be an Alaskan resident for at least a year. When an area is opened to homesteading, you go in and stake out a claim, then apply for a permit. Homesteads for settlement purposes are limited to 40 acres.

You then get title to the land in one of two ways: you "prove up" the land, or you purchase it. To "prove up" the land, you must clear a portion of it, have it surveyed, build a habitable dwelling within three years, and live on the land for not less than 25 months in a five year span. After that, the land is yours, FREE and clear!

To purchase the land, you must still clear the brush and have it surveyed. Then you have to pay fair market value for the property.

Alaska also has lotteries, where they *give away* land to qualified individuals. You have to have been a resident for a year, and you can not have received any other land grant (or homestead) from the state. Thousands of people enter these lotteries, and only a few small portions of land are given away, often in remote areas. To keep title to the land, you must make certain specified improvements in a limited period of time.

Alaska also *auctions off* a good deal of land, and has other lands regularly for sale at low prices. For information on all these programs, write to:

State of Alaska
Department of Natural Resources
PO Box 107005
Anchorage, AK 99510

Hawaii

Land sales are very rare in Hawaii, but occasionally the state auctions off some tax delinquent property. It is not likely that this land will be very cheap, but you might want to check with them anyway.

Real Property Tax Division
County of Hawaii
Department of Finance
865 Pilani St
Hilo, HI 96720

Washington

Occasionally, small tracts of land are sold by American Indians, particularly in the western states. Here's an agency in Washington State that sometimes sells land. You may want to check with the Bureau of Indian Affairs (BIA) in other states.

U.S. Department of the Interior
Bureau of Indian Affairs
Colville Indian Agency
PO Box 111
Nespelem, WA 99155

Other agencies of interest in the State of Washington (which would be worth checking in other states, too) are:

State of Washington
Department of Natural Resources
Division of Lands & Minerals
Mail Stop LB-13
Olympia, WA 98504

State of Washington
Department of Wildlife
Lands Division
600 Capitol Way N
Olympia, WA 98504

State of Washington
Department of Transportation
Land Management Branch
Highway Administration Bldg
Olympia, WA 98504

Michigan

The state of Michigan almost always has some surplus lands for sale. They have an aggressive state land management policy, and regularly buy up and dispose of state property. For more information, write to:

Lands Division
Department of Natural Resources
Box 30028
Lansing, MI 48909

Minnesota

The same is true for Minnesota:

Department of Natural Resources
Bureau of Land
Box 31,
Centennial Office Bldg
658 Cedar St
St. Paul, MN 55155

New Mexico
To find out about tax land in New Mexico, write to:

Delinquent Property Tax Bureau
Taxation and Revenue Dept
PO Box 630
Santa Fe, NM 87509

Colorado
For land leases in Colorado, contact:

Board of Land Commissioners
Department of Natural Resources
State of Colorado
620 Centennial Bldg
1313 Sherman St
Denver, CO 80203

Idaho
For information on lands in Idaho, contact:
Department of Lands
Statehouse
Boise, ID 83720

New York
For land in New York State, send off a letter to:

Office of General Services
Division of Land Utilization
Corning Tower, 26 Fl
Empire State Plaza
Albany, NY 12242

California

Now we get to dreamland — California. Most people think they can't afford land in California. But it is still possible to get it cheap through the state government or different counties.

For state surplus and excess lands and property, write to the following agencies:

Department of Water Resources
Division of Land and Right of Way
PO Box 942836
Sacramento, CA 94236

Excess Lands Branch
Division of Right of Way
Department of Transportation
PO Box 942873
Sacramento, CA 94273

For excess school lands, write to:

State Lands Commission
1807 13th St
Sacramento, CA 95814

For the purchase of unused University land, write to:

University of California
Office of the Treasurer
300 Lakeside Dr, 17th Fl
Oakland, CA 94612

And finally, for prospecting permits and mineral rights leases, you can contact these people:

State Lands Commission
245 W Broadway, Suite 425
Long Beach, CA 90802

Exceptions

There are many exceptions to the standard way that states dispose of tax lands. Each county may handle the sales different, and each state may have different laws for how property is disposed of. Don't let this stop you from using the form letters in the book, though. The differences are small enough that the people you are writing to will understand what you want, and will give you the information you need.

The following exceptions are different enough to be worth mentioning specifically.

Connecticut
This state did away with county government back in the 1960s. Any property for sale, or sold at public auction for back taxes, would be handled by the tax collector of the town where the property is located, or the town nearest the property. If you think it belongs

to one town and it turns out to belong to another, they will let you know.

New Jersey

This state does not have a county tax system. Instead, each county is divided into tax districts. To get the address and phone numbers of the districts and their tax assessors, write to:

Board of Taxation
c/o Court House
(County Seat), NJ, Zip Code

(The name of the County Seat will be in your atlas. Look for a dot inside a small circle, or a black square.)

Vermont

Tax delinquent property is handled by the separate towns. For information on such property, contact the individual town clerks in whatever town you're interested in. You don't need their names or street addresses. Just write to:

Town Clerk
(Town Name), VT, Zip Code

Maine

The State Bureau of Taxation handles the sale of tax property. For a list of such properties and the information on the next auction, write:

State Tax Assessor
Bureau of Purchases
State Office Bldg, Rm 119
Station 9
Augusta, ME 04333

- 7 -
BUYING LAND CHEAP
FROM
CITY GOVERNMENTS

Homesteading

What about homesteading in cities? You have probably heard that you can buy a house for $1.00. Yes, it's
true, but in most cases you have to promise to spend
a lot more on them. The way you get these dirt cheap
buys is through the Urban Homesteading Program.

The Urban Homesteading Program began in 1974
under direction of the Department of Housing and
Urban Development. The idea behind the program was
to improve blighted urban neighborhoods by allowing
for homesteading on unsaleable federal properties.
Briefly, the program works like this:

The Department of Housing and Urban Development
(HUD) lends money to poor people to buy homes
through the Federal Housing Administration (FHA).
When the owners fail to make their payments, FHA

pays off the mortgage and HUD forecloses on the property. This is how they get these properties in the first place.

When a city government is faced with a whole neighborhood of unoccupied, run-down houses, it can apply to HUD to start up an Urban Homesteading Program. If HUD approves the application, it transfers all of its foreclosed properties in the area to the local government. The Farmers Home Administration (FmHA) and the Veterans Administration (VA) may also transfer properties they've foreclosed on to the local government.

The total administration of Urban Homesteading Programs are the responsibility of the local governments that request them. After transferring the properties, the federal government stays out of the picture, except to insure against fraud.

Once the Urban Homesteading Program begins, the local government accepts applications from citizens for homesteading these useless houses. The applications are evaluated according to the need of the applicant for housing and the ability of the applicant to make the necessary repairs. Some cities require that applicants be residents. After narrowing down the number of applicants, a lottery is conducted to award the houses. Sometimes, thousands of people apply for only a handful of houses. The lotteries are *very* competitive.

Once the house is awarded, the new owner must agree to bring the house up to local safety standards within one year. Occasionally, federal funds are loaned to homesteaders to help them pay for the improvements. The house must be brought to local standards for safe, sanitary housing within three years. The new owner must reside in the house for five consecutive years. At the end of five years, the house is inspected. If it meets building and safety codes, ownership is transferred free and clear to the occupant.

The Urban Homesteading Program was a big success, initially. People fixed up the houses and, in many cases, neighborhoods came back to life. But the program came under severe political scrutiny a couple years ago because houses were winding up in the hands of realtors who were making handsome profits without meeting the occupancy requirements. Although the programs are still administered at the local level, HUD Regional Offices know of all programs being conducted in their jurisdictions, and will send you a listing of names and addresses of local program coordinators upon request.

For general information on the Urban Homesteading Program, write to:

Director
Urban Homesteading Program
U.S. Department of Housing and
    Urban Development
Washington, DC 20410

For specific information on currently operating programs, use the form letter in Figure 7-1 to write to the HUD Regional Office nearest to your chosen site.

Your Name
Your Street Address
Your City, State, Zip Code

Date

Urban Homesteading Director
Department of Housing and Urban
 Development
Regional Office
City, State, Zip Code

Dear Sir or Madam,

I am interested in finding out about property available through the Urban Homesteading Program.

Would you please send information about any programs in your jurisdiction, along with qualification and purchase/lease requirements?

Thank you for your assistance.

Sincerely,

(Signature)

Figure 7-1

*A sample form letter to use when writing to
HUD Regional Offices inquiring about homesteading.*

HUD Regional Offices

Alabama
Daniel Building
15 S 20th St
Birmingham 35233-2096
(205) 731-1672

Alaska
222 W 8th St
Box 64
Anchorage 99513-7537
(907) 271-3669

Arizona
One N First St
3rd Floor
Phoenix 85004-2360
(602) 261-4754

Arkansas
523 W Louisiana Suite 200
Little Rock 72201-3523
(501) 378-6375

California
1615 W Olympic Blvd
Los Angeles 90015-3801
(213) 251-7268

450 Golden Gate Av
San Francisco 94102-3448
(415) 556-3317 (Serves Nevada)

Colorado
Executive Tower
1405 Curtis St
Denver 80202-2349
(303) 844-5121 (Serves Utah, Wyoming, Montana, North Dakota and South Dakota)

Connecticut
330 Main St
Hartford 06106-1866
(203) 240-4517

District of Columbia
451 7th St NW
Washington 20410-5500
(202) 453-4527

Florida
325 W Adams St
Jacksonville 32202-4303
(904) 791-1202

Georgia
Richard B Russell Federal Building
75 Spring St SW
Atlanta 30303-3388
(404) 331-4005

Hawaii
300 Ala Moana Blvd Rm 3318
Honolulu 96850-4991
(808) 541-1327

Illinois
547 W Jackson Blvd
Chicago 60606-6765
(312) 886-0116

Indiana
151 N Delaware St
Indianapolis 46204-2526
(317) 226-6417

Kentucky
601 W Broadway
Louisville 40201-1044
(502) 582-6141

Louisiana
1661 Canal St
New Orleans 70112-0288
(504) 589-3723

Maryland
Equitable Building
10 N Calvert St
Baltimore 21202-1865
(301) 962-3723

Massachusetts
10 Causeway St
Boston 02222-1092
(617) 565-5362 (Serves Rhode Island)

Michigan
Patrick V McNamara Federal Building
477 Michigan Av
Detroit 48266-2592
(313) 226-7194

Minnesota
220 S Second St
Minneapolis-St. Paul 55401-2195
(612) 370-3025

Mississippi
Federal Building Rm 910
100 W Capitol St
Jackson 39269-1096
(601) 965-4765

Missouri
Professional Building
1103 Grand Av
Kansas City 64106-2496
(816) 374-6093

210 N Tucker Blvd
St. Louis 63101-1997
(314) 425-4363

Nebraska
Braiker/Brandeis Building 8th Fl
210 S 16th St
Omaha 68102-1622
(402) 221-3835

New Hampshire
Norris Cotton Federal Building
275 Chestnut St
Manchester 03101-2487
(603) 666-7640 (Serves Maine and Vermont)

New Jersey
Military Park Building
60 Park Place
Newark 07102-5504
(201) 877-1751

New York
Lafayette Ct 5th Fl
465 Main St
Buffalo 14203-1780
(716) 846-4557

26 Federal Plaza
New York 10278-0068
(212) 264-5028

North Carolina
415 N Edgewood St
Greensboro 27401-2107
(919) 333-5674

Ohio
New Federal Building
200 N High St
Columbus 43215-2499
(614) 469-5557

Oklahoma
200 NW 5th St
Oklahoma City 73102-3202
(405) 231-4973

Oregon
Cascade Building
520 SW 6th Av
Portland 97204-1596
(503) 294-7012 (Serves Idaho)

Pennsylvania
105 S 7th St
Philadelphia 19106-3392
(215) 597-2228

412 Old Post Office and Courthouse Bldg
7th Ave & Grant St
Pittsburgh, 15219-1906
(412) 644-5485 (Serves West Virginia)

Puerto Rico
Federico Degetau Federal Building
159 Carlos E Chardon Av Hato Rey
San Juan 00918-1804
(809) 766-5361

South Carolina
Strom Thurmond Federal Building
1835-45 Assembly St
Columbia 29201-2480
(803) 765-5328

Tennessee
710 Locust St
Knoxville 37902
(615) 549-9432

Texas
1600 Throckmorton
PO Box 2905
Fort Worth 76113-2905
(817) 885-5877

Washington Square
800 Dolorosa
San Antonio 78207-4563
(512) 229-6838

Virginia
PO Box 10170
400 N 8th St First Fl
Richmond 23240-9998
(804) 771-2853

Washington
Arcade Plaza Building
1321 Second Av
Seattle 98101-2054
(206) 442-4521

Wisconsin
Henry S Reuss Federal Plaza
310 W Wisconsin Av Ste 1380
Milwaukee 53203-2290
(414) 362-1255

Other City Lands

There are other opportunities, besides homesteading, for getting cheap land in cities. *Cities have their own real estate departments that sell surplus properties or tax delinquent properties.* In fact, some cities have so much of this property that they hold frequent auctions. The Real Property Department of the City of Boston auctions property off every week! The auctions are advertised in the leading Boston newspapers before the auction date.

Most other cities also announce their auctions well in advance in local newspapers. Some of them — like Los Angeles and San Francisco — even keep mailing lists. New York puts out a big, illustrated catalog before its auctions, which are held every three or four months and are widely advertised in area newspapers beforehand. They don't keep a mailing list, but you can get the latest catalog by writing to:

> City of New York
> Office of General Services
> Division of Real Property
> Office of Sales, Title Closings and Mortgages
> 2 Lafayette St, Room 1903
> New York, NY 10007

There are two basic types of property sold by cities:

1. Municipal property, such as abandoned firehouses, police stations, old library or school buildings, piers, jails and so forth. (It might be fun to have your own jail.)

2. Personal real estate, which includes private houses, empty lots, garages, old small commercial buildings, etc. These kinds of properties, usually one-story buildings, have sometimes been picked up very cheaply and turned into beautiful homes by people with an eye to their possibilities.

For information on surplus or tax delinquent properties to be sold by cities, use the form letter shown in Figure 7-2 on page 100.

Your Name
Your Street Address
Your City, State, Zip Code

Date

Director
Department of Real Estate
Name of City
City, State, Zip Code

Dear Sir or Madam,

Please send me information about real estate owned by your city which might be for sale. I am interested in any properties that you might be disposing of for any reason, including school property, fire or police department properties, any other buildings or land surplus to your city's needs.

I am also interested in finding out about property in your jurisdiction which might be auctioned off or otherwise sold for back taxes.

If you keep a mailing list for notification of real estate auctions or sales, would you please add my name or send me an application for adding my name to the list?

Thank you for your assistance.

Sincerely,

(Signature)

Figure 7-2

A sample form letter to use when writing to city governments in search of cheap land.

- 8 -
BUYING LAND
CHEAP IN
CANADA

Since the first edition of this book came out, the availability of inexpensive land in Canada has changed dramatically. There used to be provisions for home-steading land anywhere in Canada. Such programs are now a thing of the past. Each province may, from time to time, open remote areas of land for homesteading, but no such program is currently underway.

Further, while the Canadian provinces used to make it easy for Americans to buy Crown lands, they now make it most difficult. The policy for sale of govern-ment owned lands (called Crown lands) is set by each of the ten Canadian provinces, and not by the Cana-dian government. The basic policy that most provinces adhere to is that *they do not make Crown lands available for sale AT ALL!* This doesn't mean, how-ever, that you can't get your hands on Canadian land. Let me explain.

The Provinces

The provinces *generally* refuse to sell land through auction or tender. They are hoarding their land — and controlling its usage with all their authority. However, you can still get land. How? Through *lease*. If you see a piece of land you like, *and have a specific use in mind*, you can apply to the provincial government for a long-term lease.

If you meet the qualifications, the provincial government will lease you a parcel of Crown Land (usually at estimated market value). What are the qualifications? You must have a specific use in mind for the land (farm, home, business, etc.). You must make certain improvements to the land during the period of the lease. In most cases, you have to agree to spend a good percentage of your time living on the land. If you meet all these requirements, they *may* sell the land to you outright when the lease expires.

So you see, they really don't sell land cheap in Canada — not at the provincial level of government, anyway. Leases are arranged through the department of the provincial government which monitors the type of intended use you have in mind for the land. For example, if you want to start a farm, you contact the Department of Agriculture in the province of your choice; if you want to start a business, you contact the Department of Commerce, and so on.

When dealing with the Canadians, I recommend using a letter similar to the one shown in Figure 8-1. There is one very important aspect of your introductory letter: *DO NOT ask if they have any cheap land for sale!* Canadians seem to be very touchy about words like "cheap" and "surplus." In their view, nothing is "surplus." Also, since all land sales are for estimated market value, no land is sold "cheap." But "cheap" is a very subjective term, and "estimated market value" can be very *cheap* indeed.

Your Name
Your Street Address
Your City, State, Zip Code

Date

Canadian Agency
Street Address
City, Province, Zip Code
CANADA

Dear Sir or Madam,

I am a citizen of the United States and I am interested in leasing or purchasing Crown land in Canada.

Please send me information on the availability of Crown lands for sale or lease in your province or territory, along with the eligibility requirements for the purchase or lease of such lands.

If you keep a mailing list for notification of land sales or auctions, would you please add my name or send me an application for adding my name to the list?

Thank you for your assistance.

Sincerely,

(Signature)

Figure 8-1

A sample form letter to use when writing to Canadian governments in search of cheap land.

Saskatchewan

Saskatchewan **Agriculture**	Lands Branch	Administration Building 3085 Albert Street Regina, Canada S4S 0B1

S A L E   B Y   T E N D E R

GENERAL INFORMATION

The quarter sections of land listed herewith are now available for sale by tender from the Department of Agriculture. The quarters are grouped by Rural Municipality. Tenders will only be accepted from individuals who are able to declare that their total municipal assessment of land owned, rented and leased does not exceed an assessment of $30,000.00, and that they are a bona fide farmer.

Tender Forms and additional information may be obtained by contacting your local Ag. Rep. or Land Rep. serving your area, or by contacting Lands Branch, the Department of Agriculture in Regina.

CONDITIONS OF TENDER

1. A completed Tender Form including a signed declaration concerning the individual's eligibility to submit a tender, contained in a sealed envelope marked <u>Land Tender</u> and addressed to P.O. Box 3508, Regina, Saskatchewan, S4P 3J8, must be received by 5:00 p.m. on the closing date for tenders.

2. A certified cheque payable to Lands Branch for 5% of the highest total tender must accompany the tender.

3. Deposits of unsuccessful tenders will bear interest if not returned within 15 days of the closing date for tenders.

4. In addition to the top bid on any individual parcel, consideration will be given to the bid or bids that provide the highest aggregate price for any combination of parcels.

5. Highest, or any tender, not necessarily accepted.

6. Successful tender will have 60 days to complete the purchase.

7. Successful tender will forfeit deposit if unable to finalize purchase.

<u>DEADLINE FOR TENDERS - 5:00 p.m. April 6, 1984</u>

IMPROVEMENT CODING

H-Living accommodation; L-Livestock facilities; G-Grain storage; P-Power; W-Water; F-Fencing

R.M. 9
SW 19-2-21 W2 160 ac. -F.

R.M. 17
NW 19-4-18 W3 160 ac. -F.

R.M. 40
NW 6-6-24 W2 159 ac.

R.M. 43
SW 27-1-4 W3 158.86 ac. -F.
SE 27-1-4 W3 160 ac. -F.

R.M. 49
NE 24-4-19 W3 161 ac. -F.

R.M. 95
SE 2-12-9 W2 158 ac. -
-H,P,W,G,F,L.
NE 2-12-9 W2 160 ac.
NE 35-11-9 W2 158 ac.
NW 35-11-9 W2 158 ac. -F.
SE 35-11-9 W2 160 ac.
SW 35-11-9 W2 160 ac. -F.
NE 33-10-8 W3 157.6 ac. -F.

R.M. 99
SW 31-12-21 W2 160 ac. -G.

R.M. 153
NE 35-16-1 W2 159 ac.
SE 35-16-1 W2 160 ac.

R.M. 167
SW 31-17-14 W3 160 ac. -F.
SE 31-17-14 W3 159 ac. -F.

R.M. 256
SW 34-24-11 W3 166 ac. -F.

R.M. 286
SE 11-29-12 W3 154.97 ac.

R.M. 303
SE 22-32-2 W2 160 ac. -F.

R.M. 305
SE 11-33-7 W2 160 ac.

R.M. 317
SE 7-32-14 W3 160 ac. -F.
NW 29-32-13 W3 158 ac.

R.M. 333
SW 4-37-1 W2 160 ac. -
-H,P,W,G.
SE 32-36-1 W2 160 ac.

R.M. 335
NW 27-35-8 W2 161 ac. -F,W.

R.M. 376
Pt. NW 29-40-12 W3 131.04 ac.
(S&E of Rdy.) -F.
SE 29-40-12 W3 160 ac. -F.

R.M. 394
NE 30-45-1 W2 156.97 ac.
SW 2-43-3 W2 158.87 ac.
SE 3-43-3 W2 158.87 ac.
SW 11-43-3 W2 158.38 ac.
NW 32-43-2 W2 160 ac.
NE 32-43-2 W2 160 ac. -G.

R.M. 426
NE 2-42-11 W2 160 ac. __

R.M. 435
SW 7-43-10 W3 160 ac. -G.

R.M. 490
SW 29-50-22 W2 159 ac.

R.M. 493
SE 28-52-2 W3 160 ac.

R.M. 494
NE 8-53-6 W3 159 ac. -
-H,P,L,W,G,F.
SE 17-53-6 W3 159 ac. -G.
NE 17-53-6 W3 160 ac.
SE 8-53-6 W3 160 ac.

R.M. 496
SW 30-50-11 W3 159 ac. -
-G,W,P.
SE 25-50-12 W3 164 ac.
NE 25-50-12 W3 163 ac.
SE 36-50-12 W3 163 ac.
NW 18-52-10 W3 160 ac.
SE 19-52-10 W3 160 ac.
NW 16-52-10 W3 160 ac.

R.M. 555
NW 29-56-6 W3 159.98 ac.
SW 29-56-6 W3 160 ac.

R.M. 588
NW 14-59-20 W3 161 ac. -F.

Figure 8-2

A rare land sale announcement from
the province of Saskatchewan.

You do not have to be a Canadian citizen to buy or lease land in most provinces. However, you must show that you will use the land for the stated purpose, and you must prove that you can put in the capital necessary to make the required improvements on the land. If you already own or lease land in Canada, you can apply for an extension of your property. You can also get a lease on land if you have someone to represent you locally and to manage the land according to the lease.

In case you are interested in leasing land with the chance of an eventual purchase, the addresses of the provincial governments are listed below. They do sometimes sell parcels of land by tender or auction, as is shown in Figure 8-2, a bulletin I received from the government of Saskatchewan. Such sales are extremely rare.

Alberta
Alberta Forestry Lands & Wildlife
Public Lands Division
Petroleum Plaza — South Tower
9915 108 St
Edmonton, Alberta T5K 2C9 CANADA

British Columbia
Ministry of Crown Lands
Land Policy Branch
3rd Floor, 4000 Seymour Pl
Victoria, BC V8V 1X5 CANADA

Manitoba
Lands Branch
Department of Natural Resources
1495 St. James St
Winnipeg, Manitoba R3H 0W9 CANADA

New Brunswick
Crown Lands Branch
Department of Natural Resources
PO Box 6000
Fredericton, NB E3B 5H1 CANADA

Newfoundland
Department of Environment and Lands
Eastern Regional Office
PO Box 8700
St. John's, Newfoundland A1B 4J6 CANADA

Nova Scotia
Department of Lands and Forests
Torrington Pl, Suite 302
780 Windmill Rd
Dartmouth, Nova Scotia B3B 1T3 CANADA

Ontario
Land Management Branch
Ministry of Natural Resources
99 Wellesley St W
Toronto, Ontario M7A 1W3 CANADA

Prince Edward Island
Land Use Commission
Box 2000
Charlottetown, P.E.I. C1A 7N8 CANADA

Quebec
Ministre de l'Energie et des Ressources
200, chemin Sainte-Foy
6ieme etage
Quebec, QC G1R 4X7 CANADA

Saskatchewan
Parks and Lands Branch
Dept of Parks & Renewable Resources
3211 Albert St
Regina, Saskatchewan S4S 5W6 CANADA

- or -

Saskatchewan Rural Development
Walter Scott Bldg
3085 Albert St
Regina, Saskatchewan S4S 0B1 CANADA

One exception to the tight hold over Crown land is the extreme northern territories of Canada. You may be able to lease or purchase land there with relative ease. For more information, write to:

Indian and Northern Affairs Canada
Land Resources
PO Box 1500
Yellowknife, Northwest Territories X1A 2R3
CANADA

Indian and Northern Affairs Canada
200 Range Road
Whitehorse, Yukon Territory Y1A 3V1 CANADA

Does all this mean that there is no cheap land available in Canada anymore? *NO!* It just means that the *provinces* are being tight with Crown land. They want indefinite control over the usage of all the land within their jurisdiction. In fact, for commercial ventures, *they will not even consider selling land — only leasing it!* Apparently, the Canadian governments feel they can't lose if they are perpetual landlords, and nobody can buy property outright.

The Cities

But there is some cheap land available for *purchase* in Canada. Where? In the municipalities. It is the municipalities that collect property taxes, and they *do* sell off tax-foreclosed property. The process is very similar to that for city and county governments in the United States. The land is sold either through auction or tender (sealed bids). Notification of sales must appear in local newspapers several months before the auction.

All tender bids must be accompanied by a deposit equal to some percentage of the minimum bid (say 10%). The land goes to the highest bidder, with one exception. People are allowed to bid on a group of parcels with one bid. If that single bid is higher than the total of the highest bids on each separate parcel, then the whole group goes to the single bidder. The municipality cannot sell the land for less than the taxes due. The prior owner has one year after the date of sale to pay the back taxes and reclaim the land.

If no one offers the minimum bid, then the government can privately sell off the land at a later date for whatever it can get. *This is probably your best bet for getting cheap land* in Canada! Because the second sale of the land doesn't have to be public, you won't have to compete with other bidders. If the land has been unsold for a long time, it could have simply been forgotten. Your letter to the municipality could jar loose a real gem!

So, the most likely way to get cheap land in Canada is to buy tax foreclosed property from municipal governments. You can get a complete listing of municipal governments in Canada (and their address) by writing for the booklet "Municipal Directory" from:

Ontario Government Bookstore
Publications Ontario
880 Bay St, 5th Fl
Toronto, Ontario M7A 1N8 CANADA

The directory costs $8.10 (with tax, Canadian dollars) as of this writing. Make checks payable to the Treasurer of Ontario. You may also order the directory by telephone if you have a VISA or MasterCard. The toll-free number is 1-800-668-9938.

For general information about the land policies of the Canadian governments, write for the free booklet, "An Overview of Crown Land Management in Canada," available from:

Sustainable Development
State of Environmental Reporting Branch
Corporate Policy Group
Environment Canada
351 St. Joseph Blvd
Hull, Quebec K1A 0E7 CANADA

The best source of information on cheap land available in Canada is the *Ontario Gazette*, which publishes lists of tax delinquent property on the first Saturday of each month. Their list describes the size and location of the property, and shows the amount of tax in arrears and the date, time and place of the sale. For a single copy, send $1.00 to:

The Ontario Gazette
5th Floor, 880 Bay St
Toronto, Ontario M7A 1N8 CANADA

Another good source for land is the *Crown Land Marketing Catalog*, published by Crown Publications. This catalog contains a listing of properties available for immediate sale from the Ministry of Crown Lands. The catalog is updated quarterly. There are generally no citizenship restrictions on purchase of these lands.

The catalog costs $21.75 (Canadian) and is available from:

Crown Publications, Inc.
546 Yates St
Victoria, B.C. V8W 1K8 CANADA

- 9 -
OTHER WAYS TO BUY LAND CHEAP

The ways to buy land cheap are limited only by your imagination and persistence. There is land available in every state in the U.S. and in most cities. The land that is cheap is inexpensive because it's out of the way, or because very few people know that it exists and is for sale, or because the seller is willing to take an extremely steep discount for the land.

The key to finding cheap land is to *keep digging!* If you want to buy land in a certain area, then research *all* your options. Send letters to county treasurers for tax land, talk to mortgage bankers and real estate agents in the areas where you want to live, contact other government agencies that may own land in the area, and just go through the countryside looking for interesting property. The land will go to the persistent.

We've already talked about getting cheap land from the federal government, state governments, city and county governments, but there are more places to check. Aside from tax collectors, it seems that nearly every government agency has control over some surplus land. Let's look at a few examples.

Transportation & Highway Departments

State highway departments own thousands of acres of land. They buy land that they might build roads on, and they have land where roads are no longer being serviced. These lands are sometimes disposed of. If you address a letter to your state highway department asking for any surplus lands in the area you want to live in, you might make a surprising find.

State departments of transportation (if this is separate from the highway department) also own large tracts of land. They own old railroad rights of way, waterfront land held for possible shipping use, and even land from 100 years ago when they used to build canals all over the place. A letter to these folks could turn up an interesting piece of forgotten property.

One of the best examples of cheap land we have ever seen came from the Washington State Department of Transportation. The department holds regular auctions of surplus lands. The auctions are conducted by sealed bid with a 10% deposit required and, unlike other land sellers, *the state will finance some purchases on a real estate contract.* A packet for the November, 1990, auction included the following parcels: 0.03 acre parcel for $50, a 0.12 acre parcel for $50, a 0.30 acre parcel for $50 and a 0.11 acre parcel for $10. That's right, ten dollars.

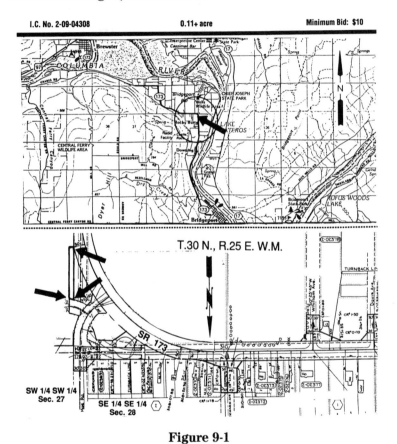

Figure 9-1

*A $10.00 piece of property available from
the Washington State Department of Transportation.*

The map for the $10 parcel is shown in Figure 9-1. It's a little strip of a thing, next to the highway, measuring 15 feet by 230 feet. It has electric power, telephone, is level and covered with brush and grasses (this is an arid part of Washington State). The property is zoned "Rural, Agricultural," so you probably couldn't build a house without a re-zone. But it might be an ideal place to park an RV or just plant some wildflowers. At a price of $10.00, who could pass this up?

Many county governments, especially in metropolitan areas, also have highway departments. These agencies can have a great deal of autonomy, since they have an independent source of funding through gasoline taxes. For this reason, they may handle their own surplus land sales, rather than letting some other bureaucratic agency dispose of their unwanted land. This is the perfect example of how persistent, thorough digging may yield a real find.

Other Government Departments

There are state departments of natural resources, fisheries and wildlife departments, forestry departments, the department of game, the list goes on and on. Nearly every state has one or more departments that manage some property. These departments may sell off parcels of unused land, or may lease it at low prices for long terms. They are certainly worth canvassing if you are set on living in a certain area and haven't yet found cheap land.

Some of these departments may seem ridiculous, like state Boards of Education, but that's exactly what makes them good places to try. Since no one would ever think of asking about land from some of these places, no one does. When no one is asking about the land, when no one knows about it, that's when you will find parcels at the best bargains. Why? Because most government agencies sell land for "fair market value." If nobody else knows about the land besides you and the agency, then *YOU are the market* and what you're willing to pay is "fair market value."

Other agencies to check are those that deal with water and sewage. Other utilities like the phone company and the gas company and the electric company and the agencies that regulate them may have land. Unused land often gets forgotten in these places. Your letter or phone call could knock something loose. Don't pass up these opportunities in your search for cheap land.

Homesteading

What about homesteading? Sorry, but that frontier is closed. The dream is over — except for homesteading in cities under the HUD program, as discussed in the chapter on cities. The Homestead Act of 1862 was done away with in 1976. Homesteading in Alaska was continued until the Alaska Lands Bill passed Congress in 1980. Homesteading in Alaska was discontinued until 1984, when the state government started its own program. Today, you must be a resident to homestead in Alaska, but the opportunity still exists. For more information on homesteading in Alaska, see the State Government section of this book.

Distressed Sales

Governments aren't the only ones that sell land cheap. For a variety of reasons, banks, finance companies, auction houses and private individuals sell off property at bargain prices. When a marriage ends in divorce, property is sometimes sold for less than market value in order to quickly settle the claims. When businesses go bankrupt, creditors will sell off the assets, often as fast as possible. Someone unable to make their mortgage payments may sell their home to avoid foreclosure. If the real estate market is sluggish, these distress sales can result in exceptional bargains.

Foreclosures

Let's start with the case of someone unable to make their mortgage payments. Maybe they lost their job or came down with an illness or for some other reason aren't able to make their payments. These people will often be willing to sell at whatever the market brings to avoid foreclosure, even if the market is temporarily very bad. You can find out about foreclosure actions by reading the legal notices in the newspaper serving the county seat. Banks are required to give several weeks of printed notice before they can foreclose. This is your chance to find the owner and make him an offer he can't refuse.

If the bank has already foreclosed, good deals could still be in the making. Banks, like county tax assessors, don't want to hold onto property for long. Their business is making loans and mortgages, not land speculation or renting. They may want to dispose of the property as quickly as possible.

When you are visiting one of your target locations, look in at the mortgage departments of the town's banks. Do they have any foreclosed property coming up for auction soon? In most cases, the bank is legally required to give notice of sale in the local paper. But notice is often small print legalese, and few people know about the sale.

Also ask the banker if he has any bank-owned property for sale. If the bank tried to auction off a foreclosed piece of property and no one made a satisfactory bid, the bank will usually buy the property itself to protect its mortgage. *This property does not have to be sold at public auction! This is the kind of property that no one knows is available for sale!* You may be able to cut a deal with the bank on this property. Remember, they want to get rid of it and they may even give you an irresistible deal on financing just to get it off their hands!

Divorce

Divorce is another common reason for selling property at distress prices. One of the couple may have won a property settlement and own the property in full, but want to dispose of it. In many cases, the property must be sold so that the proceeds can be divided between the partners. Divorce actions must also appear in the legal notice section of newspapers. By scanning these, you could get in on a good deal before the property is made available publicly.

Death

Untimely death also makes for good property deals, though the cause of such finds is sad. When property is owned by a married couple, and one spouse dies, the property usually goes to the survivor. The surviving spouse may not want to continue living in the house. The upkeep might be too much to handle alone. He or she may want to move away quickly, and your offer to purchase the property at the current market price or below could be an act of mercy. If the market is currently slow, you could make a handsome profit when things turn around.

Bankruptcy

Good deals are also in the air when a business goes bankrupt. The creditors want to dispose of the assets and get their cash back as quickly as possible. Most creditors don't care to hold the property and won't wait for the market to improve. Again, you can find out about bankruptcies through legal notices and contact the creditors to find out about how the debtor's assets will be disposed of.

The key to foreclosure and distress sales is to keep your eyes peeled on the legal announcements. You must realize that there are often forced property sales that go along with most legal actions. These kinds of sales happen regardless of market conditions, and true bargains are there for the taking — for those who have a sharp eye and the persistence to follow these leads.

Prospecting for Cheap Land

There are still other ways and places to buy land cheap, but you have to go after them. Sometimes you have to make a real effort — write letters, ask questions, track it down, but it is there *and it can be bought cheap* — if you go about it the right way.

Just what is the right way? There is no single right way to get what you want, but there is one main thing to keep in mind when you're dealing with people who don't know you, and especially non-city people: *you* are the stranger. This sets you apart from the beginning. But you can close this gap by simple courtesy and sincerity. If you come on like a sharpie, the people who can help you will just clam up and you won't get the time of day out of them.

Okay, with that in mind, suppose you are driving through a rural area and you spot an old building. It could be a barn, or warehouse, or abandoned factory. It might have been used as all three at some time or other. But now it is empty and in pretty bad shape because it hasn't been used for anything for some time. It is just sitting there. It might look like an eyesore to the locals, but that's not what it looks like to you. Maybe under the rotting roof you see the solid construction, and the large loft and floor space. In your mind's eye, you can see a beautiful home or studio. This talent to see what something *could be* when it is fixed up is definitely in your favor. Keep an especially keen eye out for fire damaged property that is not too far gone.

What do you do next? Ask. Whom to ask? The nearest neighbor, or the storekeeper, or if they don't know anything, go to the town clerk in the nearest town and ask him or her. If they don't know, go to the County Recorder at the County Courthouse. But you probably would not have to go that far. A neighbor could likely tell you something.

You might find that the building *belongs* to the neighbor who never thought of selling because nobody ever asked about it before. Other possibilities: the building might be part of a tract that includes an abandoned rock quarry. Or maybe the property belongs to an absentee owner who would be happy to dump it for a low, low price.

The owner could be a widow who would like to sell out and move south, but hasn't been able to swing it and selling the building could make the difference. Or it could belong to an old couple who need the money for medical expenses, or who want to go into a nursing home and don't want another piece of taxable property to worry about.

Checklist

Here is something else that will help a lot when you're just roaming around looking for a place: *Keep a checklist.* Here are some questions you can put on it:

☐ How much is the property?

☐ How much is the down payment?

☐ Will the present owner hold a mortgage?

☐ How much are the property taxes?

☐ How much are the school taxes?

☐ How much are the road taxes?

☐ Are there access or easement problems?

☐ How far is it to the nearest work center?

You don't have to stand the nearest neighbor against a tree and shoot these questions at him, but do try to find out some of the answers while you are also checking out the roof, plumbing, etc.

- 10 -

LOST LAND

There are a couple different ways land may become "lost" or unclaimed, besides being lost for taxes. This chapter will briefly touch upon these other ways.

Land Lost in History

As pioneers settled the vast American continent, they homesteaded and developed communities and towns. Prospectors patented their mining claims and large companies such as railroads were granted huge amounts of land for right of ways and other developments. In those days, land was of seemingly limitless supply, and was therefore relatively cheap. Settlements often failed and ghost towns were not uncommon, as the people simply packed up and moved to where the grass looked greener. Their land and possessions were abandoned.

If the records office burned or was moved, records of land ownership were sometimes lost or destroyed. Although federal land offices held the records of transfers of land to private ownership from the government, subsequent sales or transfers were (and still are) only recorded at the recording office of the local government.

These local governments were dependent upon taxes of various sorts, including real estate property taxes — their basic means of support. This tax served to provide a listing of property and its owners recorded in the jurisdiction. Often, the local assessor listed only the property he wished to. Land sometimes remained untaxed if government deeds were delayed or not recorded. Often, land was not listed for taxes if it was considered to be of no value.

In areas where the local assessors have not combed the (usually) remote government lands status records and taken the tedious time to compare these records with the local plat books, there is a possibility that some land in these rural areas has an unclaimed, untaxed status: land "lost" in history.

Land Lost in Conveyance

Parcels were split off and sold as land changed ownership. Frequently, such parcels were sold according to geographical convenience, since government surveys were rectangular and, except for land along navigable water, did not run on natural boundaries. Splits like these required "metes and bounds," or irregular surveys. Sometimes just the visual description of the boundaries of the parcels sold were all that was used. The boundaries often changed with trails across the land or with the changing of stream or river channels. At times, land would be left out of a deed and lost to the tax rolls and subsequent owners.

"Lost" land of this kind is usually in small parcels, but often in a good location with road or river frontage. Unless someone comes along to point out a discrepancy, local assessors will usually assume that their current listings are correct. It is because of this that land sometimes has become "lost" in conveyance.

- 11 -

INSIDE TIPS

Okay, now let's turn the lights down low and get to the real nitty-gritty: the inside tips you've been waiting for. We have mentioned Daniels County, Montana. Here are some of the other counties with numerous lots under a hundred bucks and houses for a few hundred dollars. In listing the addresses, I am putting the county seat under the county name.

County Treasurer
County Court House
Prairie County
Terry, MT 59349

County Treasurer
County Court House
Roosevelt County
Wolf Point, MT 59201

County Auditor
County Court House
Divide County
Crosby, ND 58730

County Clerk
County Court House
Ozark County
Gainesville, MO 65655

In Divide County, we could have bought 50 lots for $189.00 total price! In Mellette County, White River, South Dakota, we could have bought half the town of Wood for less than $1,500.00!

And that is just the tip of the iceberg as you will soon find out when you start snooping around on your own — writing letters, asking questions, studying the atlas.

Here are my "inside" suggestions on general areas that are really good bets for buying land cheap. Remember, we told you earlier in this book that if you were interested in an area to blanket it with inquiry letters — at least six counties in all directions. So you don't have to limit your ambitions to my Best Bet List, but it is a good starting point. *Here they are:*

- Western and northeastern New York State
- Northwestern Pennsylvania
- Southern Illinois
- Southern Missouri
- Northern Arkansas
- West central Mississippi

- Central Alabama
- Northern Michigan
- Northwestern Minnesota
- Western Colorado
- Northeastern California

A final note: This is the fourth edition of ***How to Buy Land Cheap.*** Because real estate prices in general will climb as the population grows, and because the urge to own property is so fundamental to the human spirit, the desire to find cheap land will not go away. We have been astounded by how strong that urge is, and we are happy to have helped so many find the land that they yearn for.

If you have had success finding cheap land using our book, please write to us in care of the publisher, so that this information can be passed on in future editions of this book. If you'd like, tell us about how you found your land, how you bought it, and anything interesting or surprising that happened along the way. Tell us what you've done with your land or what you plan to do: build a house, park an RV, plant flowers, whatever. Best of all, we'd love to have a photo to share with future readers. You can reach us at the following address:

How to Buy Land Cheap
c/o Loompanics Unlimited
PO Box 1197
Port Townsend, WA 98368

- 12 -
OTHER
HELPFUL
INFORMATION

A free list of publications on farming, livestock, forestry, soil and so forth can be ordered from:

U.S. Department of Agriculture
Washington, DC 20250

A good way to get the lowdown on land you haven't seen is to order terrain maps from the U.S. Geological Survey. Write to these guys, specify what states you're interested in, and they will send you price information on maps:

Department of the Interior
U.S. Geological Survey
Reston, VA 22092

A great source for information is *The Personal Choice Connection.* This publication is a guide to other publications and research materials that will help you find real estate all over the world. For more information, write to:

> The Personal Choice Connection
> 252 Carlton Club Dr
> Piscataway, NJ 08854

For a variety of information on America's best small communities and the rigors of rural living, write to:

> Relocation Research
> PO Box 1122
> Sierra Madre, CA 91025

Other Useful Publications

Rand-McNally Road Atlas (paperback).

Rand-McNally Standard Reference Map & Guide (one for each state you're interested in).

How to Find Real Estate Bargains, by Phillip Fry. Published by Tax Information Center.

How to Cash In on Little-Known Real Estate Investment Opportunities, by Samuel T. Barash. Published by Prentice-Hall, Inc.

Foreclosures: How to Profitably Invest in Distressed Properties, by Andrew J. McLean. Published by Contemporary Books.

How to Make Money Fast Speculating in Distressed Properties, by John V. Kamin. Published by Forecaster Publications.

How to Buy Land, by L. John Wachtel. Published by Sterling Publishing Company.

Little Known Facts & Secrets About Real Estate, by Earl C. Carlisle. Published by Carlisle Industries.

Save Thousands When You Buy or Sell Your Home, by John D. Bowers. Published by J.D. Bowers.

Secrets of a Professional Home Buyer, by William W. Bell. Published by Worldwide Publishing Corporation.

Lower Your Real Estate Taxes, by Robert G. Johnson. Published by Walker & Company.

Five Acres and Independence, by M.G. Cains. Published by Dover.

Finding and Fixing Old Houses (for Fun and Fortune), by B.E. and E.F. Harris. Published by Harris House.

The Land Buyer's Handbook, by Robert C. Malmgren. Published by Land Systems International, Inc.

Real Estate Sales Handbook, by the National Association of Realtors. Published by Charles Scribner's Sons.

Almost Free Land, by Phillip P. Karagan. Published by Phillip P. Karagan.

Real Estate Tax Sale Manual, by Thomas Hendricks. Published by Tax Property Investor.

Save Your Home: Avoid Foreclosure and Make A Profit, by Steven L. Porter. Published by Java Publishing Co.

How to Make It When You're Cash Poor, by Hollis Norton. Published by Simon and Schuster.

Buying Right, by John Schaub. Published by Pro Serv Corp.

The Alternative Land Acquisition Handbook, by Timothy Traquair. Published by Ridgehaven.

Goldmining in Foreclosure Properties, by Val Cabot. Published by Impact Publishing Co.

Distress Property: How to Buy It in California, by Bill Greene. Published by Bill Greene.

Where to Find It

Maps

Forest Service Maps	Regional or District Forest Service Office cartography supplier.
BLM Maps	Regional BLM and Forest Service Offices.
Land Status Maps	U.S. Geological Survey Offices or engineers, surveyors and cartographers.
Topographical Quads	Field Service and BLM Offices, engineers, surveyors and cartographers.
Ownership Maps	County Assessor's Office.

Other Items

Delinquent tax list . . . . County Treasurer's Office

Deeds, Court Orders,
Mortgages, Liens . . . . County Clerk and
Recorder's Office

Probate records . . . . Court Clerk

Blank deed forms . . . . Office supply stores

Original survey field notes . . . . Regional BLM Office

Assessment lists . . . . County Assessor's Office

Help with interpretation
of local real estate laws . . . . State Real Estate
Manual for brokers
and salesmen.

- 13 -
GLOSSARY
OF
TERMS

Abstract. An Abstract of Title is a history of ownership of the property.

Access. The right to enter or come onto.

Assessed Valuation. The value placed on a piece of property by government for the purpose of taxation.

Certificate of Title. Contains the legal description of both a house and land, and proves the ownership of the house.

Cloud on the Title. Anything which would affect or impair the title.

Conveyance. The means by which title to real estate is transferred from owner to owner.

Deed. A written instrument in which real estate is transferred or conveyed.

Distress Property. Owners are in jeopardy of losing their equity.

Easement. The right to use the land other than as a tenant, for a specific purpose.

Foreclosure. A forced sale of property in order to collect on a mortgage.

Grantee. The buyer; the person to whom the real estate is conveyed.

Grantor. The seller; the person who conveys, by deed, the real estate.

Legal Description. A description sufficient to locate and identify the property.

Lien. A claim on someone else's property as security for the payment of a just debt.

Marketable Title. A title free from any encumbrances or clouds, which a court would compel a purchaser to accept.

Metes and Bounds. Describing the measurement and boundaries of land using geographical characteristics.

Plat. A map, plan or chart of a town, city, section, subdivision, etc., showing the location and boundaries of pieces of property.

Plat Book. A public record of various plats in a specific area.

Quiet Title. A court action brought to remove a cloud on the title and establish the title.

Quit Claim Deed. A deed in which the grantor transfers whatever interest he has in the property without warranty.

Tax Deed. The type of deed you receive when you buy property for back taxes.

Title. The total evidence which proves ownership.

Title Insurance. An insurance policy against a defective title.

Title Search. Usually mandatory before a house is sold. The examination of ownership papers filed at the courthouse to make sure there are no liens on the property.

Warranty Deed. A deed which the grantor agrees to protect against any claimant.

YOU WILL ALSO WANT TO READ: